WALKING IN THE AUVERGNE

About the Authors

Carl McKeating and Rachel Crolla, seen here in the Montagne Bourbonnaise, hail from Bradford, and began their hiking careers in the Yorkshire Dales and the Lake District. They went on to walk and climb all over Europe, exploring all the major mountain ranges. In 2007, Rachel became the first woman to climb to the highest point of every country in Europe. The couple's resulting guidebook, *Europe's High Points*, was published by Cicerone in 2009. It was while writing this book that Carl and Rachel first visited the Auvergne. They liked it so much that they bought a dilapidated old house there, and between renovation nightmares they hiked all over the Auvergne's four *départements*. The couple's first child, Heather, was born during the writing of *Walking in the Auvergne* and Rachel bravely completed some of the routes while 7½ months pregnant.

Carl and Rachel spend much of their free time rock climbing, and have recently completed another tick list with Ken Wilson's *Classic Rock*. They have also travelled extensively in the mountain ranges of North America.

WALKING IN THE AUVERGNE

by Rachel Crolla and Carl McKeating

2 POLICE SQUARE, MILNTHORPE, CUMBRIA LA7 7PY
www.cicerone.co.uk

© Rachel Crolla and Carl McKeating 2013
First edition 2013
ISBN: 978 1 85284 651 0

Printed by KHL Printing, Singapore
A catalogue record for this book is available from the British Library.
All photographs are by the authors unless otherwise stated.

The routes of the GR®, PR® and GRP® paths in this guide have been reproduced with the permission of the Fédération Française de la Randonnée Pédestre holder of the exclusive rights of the routes. The names GR®, PR® and GRP® are registered trademarks. ©FFRP 2013 for all GR®, PR® and GRP® paths appearing in this work.

Acknowledgements

Thanks are due to Casey McKeating for helping us with an alternative route in the Monts Dore chapter. Thanks also to Rory McKeating who is partially responsible for our decision to purchase a home in the Auvergne and the ensuing years of DIY.

Advice to Readers

While every effort is made by our authors to ensure the accuracy of guidebooks as they go to print, changes can occur during the lifetime of an edition. If we know of any, there will be an Updates tab on this book's page on the Cicerone website (www.cicerone.co.uk), so please check before planning your trip. We also advise that you check information about such things as transport, accommodation and shops locally. Even rights of way can be altered over time. We are always grateful for information about any discrepancies between a guidebook and the facts on the ground, sent by email to info@cicerone.co.uk or by post to Cicerone, 2 Police Square, Milnthorpe LA7 7PY, United Kingdom.

Front cover: Puy de Sancy from the spectacular Grand Horseshoe (Walk 22)

CONTENTS

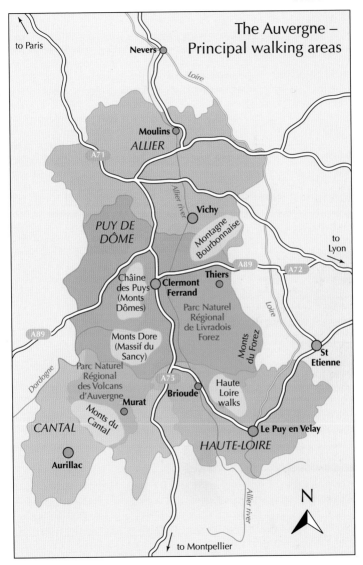

The Auvergne –
Principal walking areas

to Paris

Nevers

Loire

Moulins
ALLIER

A71

Allier river

Vichy

PUY DE DÔME

to Lyon

Montagne Bourbonnaise

A89   A72

Châine des Puys (Monts Dômes)   **Clermont Ferrand**   **Thiers**

A89

Monts Dore (Massif du Sancy)

Parc Naturel Régional de Livradois Forez

Loire

Monts du Forez

Parc Naturel Régional des Volcans d'Auvergne

A75

Brioude

Haute Loire walks

St Etienne

Dordogne

Murat

Monts du Cantal

Le Puy en Velay

CANTAL

HAUTE-LOIRE

Aurillac

Allier river

N

to Montpellier

7

Map Key

═══ A17 ═══	motorway	Ȣ	campsite
═══ N17 ═══	main road	†	cross
═══ D17 ═══	minor road	⁂	wind farm
····················	path	cliff/crag	cliff/crag
───────	route	scree	scree
●●●●●●●●●●●●●●●●●	alt route	●	waterfall
─ ─ ─ ─ ─ ─ ─	GR route	□	reservoir
····················	seasonal river	=	bridge
	river/lake	⋈	col
= = = =	tunnel	⋔	wooded area
━━●━━	railway	⋏	pylon
├──────┤	cable car	▱	dam
○	spot height	castle	castle
▲	peak	church	church
✝	peak with summit cross	P	parking
■	isolated building	SF	start/finish
□	large rock/menhir/dolmen	→	route direction
	urban area		
◉	city, town or village		
●	hamlet		

Contour colour key

	0m – 400m		1100m – 1200m
	400m – 500m		1200m – 1300m
	500m – 600m		1300m – 1400m
	600m – 700m		1400m – 1500m
	700m – 800m		1500m – 1600m
	800m – 900m		1600m – 1700m
	900m – 1000m		1700m – 1800m
	1000m – 1100m		1800m – 1900m

Starting up the Elancèze (Walk 10)

Chastelle sur Murat from the Chapelle de St Antoine (Walk 5)

INTRODUCTION

The ridge between Puy Mary (right) and Puy de Peyre Arse (left) from Puy de Niermont

The massive Auvergne region lies deep in the heart of France. A land forged by the furnaces of ancient volcanic eruptions, the Auvergne evolved over millennia to provide a wealth of unique and spectacular walking territory. From the Christmas pudding-shaped domes of the volcanic Châine des Puys (also known as the Monts Dômes) to the high steep ridges of the Cantal supervolcano, the Auvergne has hills to suit every hiker. The ancient tracks, high gentian meadows and immaculate forests of rural Livradois Forez and Montagne Bourbonnaise are also a rambler's paradise. The Auvergne's charming historic villages, castles and churches are interspersed with picturesque hamlets, pastoral valleys and lofty cattle pastures. Unspoilt volcanic lakes nestle within pine forests and languid rivers trace their sinuous courses through beech copses.

While not advertising its charms as widely as the honeypots of the Alps and Pyrenees, the Auvergne encompasses the major part of the Massif Central and provides a stunning breadth of hiking and volcanic scenery covering an area of 25,000km^2, with thousands of waymarked paths. The majority of the terrain is not a playground for alpine supermen but offers a variety of walking well within the scope of those accustomed to hiking in Britain. The Auvergne is easily accessible to the holidaymaker and lends itself to being explored by the day walker.

The accessible height (from 1000m to 1900m) of the volcanic peaks in the Cantal and Monts Dore means there are interesting objectives for those seeking both easy and challenging excursions in the mountains. In contrast to the Cantal and Sancy ridges, the distinctive pimple-like hills of the Monts Dômes rise individually to form a bumpy 'join the dots' picture. These are ideal for shorter hikes. To the northeast the gentler hills and vales of the Montagne Bourbonnaise serve up an unforgettable slice of quintessential rural France, where the tranquil beauty remains unspoilt. This area boasts picturesque medieval villages and superb paths through wooded glades, blooming hedgerowed fields and summits with attractive rocky outcrops. Further south, the Livradois Forez and Velay offer a network of trails through pristine forests, connecting the fascinating religious and historic monuments of the region.

The people of the Auvergne owe the name of their region to the Celts. The Celtic emblem for the area was a tree called a *vergne* (an alder) and the name for the province grew from this. The modern region is split into four *départements*: Allier in the north, Haute-Loire to the southeast, Puy de Dôme to the west and Cantal to the southwest. Much of the latter two are covered by the Parc Naturel Régional des Volcans – the largest nature reserve in France. Do not be alarmed, none of the volcanoes are

Through huge open wheatfields on Walk 38 – Châtel Montagne and the Puy de Roc

Woodcutting in the Montagne Bourbonnaise

active – in fact the eruptions that formed the unique landscape took place many thousands of years ago.

The Auvergne is one of the most sparsely populated regions of Europe, let alone France. Major centres include the stately spa town of Vichy, Clermont-Ferrand – one of France's oldest cities – and the magical le Puy en Velay. It is an area steeped in history and proud of its regional identity and produce. The Auvergne boasts its own dialect and regional language – a form of Occitan called Auvergnat. Over half of the Auvergne's inhabitants claim to be able to understand Auvergnat in spite of the fact that UNESCO's *Red Book of Endangered Languages* lists it as severely endangered.

The Auvergne is traditionally a farming region where the pace of life seems relaxed and untouched by modern hustle and bustle. Tourism is, however, on the increase and although you are likely to have many of the routes in this book to yourselves, this may soon change. An influx of visitors, particularly from the Benelux countries, has allowed the plentiful *auberges*, *chambres de hôtes* and village campsites in the region to flourish.

HISTORY

Stone Age man has left his traces in the Auvergne, and several Neolithic dolmens and menhirs are visited on the walks in this book. The Auvergne is known to have been populated in

13

the Lower Paleolithic period over a million years ago. The archeological site at Chilhac in the Haute-Loire (near Walk 34) has uncovered some of the oldest evidence of humans in Europe, as well as skeletons of Auvergnat mastodons. The volcanic geology of the area is ideal for preserving these remains. A famous Neolithic site at Glozel (near Walks 36 and 37) has been the subject of some controversy because of the anachronistic writing and harpoon carvings found there.

The Gallic province of Arverni was named after the Celtic tribe of the Arvernes. The fearsome Vercingétorix, who features in the Asterix books, became king in 52BC. He managed to take over after his father was killed by rival tribesmen who did not want hereditary secession. Vercingétorix had the cunning strategy of holding the families of the renegade tribesmen hostage until they swore loyalty. The Arvernes became rich due to the plentiful natural resources of the area and the easily defendable mountainous territory. Vercingétorix famously defeated Julius Caesar in a battle which took place at Gergovia, near to Clermont-Ferrand. His impressive statue can be found in the city today. The Arverni victory was short-lived, however: the Romans defeated them at Alésia, and imprisoned Vercingétorix in Rome. The Romans then built Augusto Nemetum, which became Clermont-Ferrand, and the Roman temple of Mercury on Puy de Dôme, which is visited on Walk 16.

The medieval castle of Polignac on its volcanic plinth

From the Roman era to the Bourbons

Auvergne briefly passed into the hands of the Visigoths in the late 5th century under King Euric before passing to the Francs, and then the Aquitaines. The medieval period was blighted by plagues as well as by bloody invasions of Saracens and Normans, who burnt the region's capital – now called Clermont-Ferrand – to the ground. Warring religious factions continued the unsettled period before the Aquitaines invented the Countship of Auvergne and renamed the capital Montferrand. The counts were assisted by various Auvergnat nobles including the Viscounts of Murat (Walk 5) and Polignac. The Middle Ages were also notable for the rise of the Auvergne abbeys such as Chaise-Dieu (Walk 29) and the Romanesque art in the churches at Orcival (Walk 18) and St Nectaire (Walk 27).

In the 12th century the Auvergne came under the rule of Henry II of England when he married Eleanor of Aquitaine, who was heiress of the region. There ensued a period of French–English war and Auvergne nobles divided their support between Richard the Lionheart and Philippe-Auguste of France. The French king was unhappy with this rebellion and deposed the Auvergnat Count Guy II by laying siege to the château at Tournoël (Walk 21). Auvergne was consequently split into four political divisions. Prosperous times for the region came to an end with constant conflicts including the French victory in the Hundred Years War, and the advent of the Black Death, which decimated the Auvergnat population in the 14th century. The Bourbonnaise dynasty were the principal rulers of Auvergne in the 15th century but the province was annexed to the French crown again in the 16th century. In 1665 Louis XIV set up a special court in Clermont that executed various Auvergne nobles who were convicted of atrocities.

Into the 20th century

The modern Auvergne *départements* of Haute-Loire, Allier, Cantal and Puy de Dôme came into being in 1790 with the advent of the Republic. Industrialisation in the 19th century meant Clermont flourished as the home of inventor Edouard Michelin and his tyre company. When France fell to the Germans in 1940, Marshal Philippe Pétain set up the Vichy government in that city, collaborating with the Axis powers. The Vichy regime retained power in unoccupied southern France until the whole country was subjected to full German rule in 1942. The Vichy government aided the Nazis in rounding up Jews and other 'undesirables' and there was bitter conflict between the Resistance and those supporting the government's stance.

The Resistance movement in Auvergne grew at this time, with *maquis* (rural guerrilla bands) hiding out in the high mountains and sabotaging German operations. Two battles took place in the Auvergne in 1944 before the eventual Allied victory, when General Charles de Gaulle returned from exile to form a new French government and 'purges' against Nazi collaborators began. Unfortunately for the Auvergne, the name of Vichy is still synonymous to many people with Nazi sympathisers.

The modern administrative region of the Auvergne was established under the Fourth Republic in 1972.

VOLCANOES

One of the most exciting opportunities of a visit to the Auvergne is the chance to walk in among the unique giant sleeping volcanoes of the region. The Parc Naturel Régional des Volcans d'Auvergne (Auvergne Volcanoes Natural Park) covers nearly 400,000 hectares and is the largest protected area in France, stretching 120km from north to south.

The Auvergne volcanoes fall into three categories.

- Scoria (cinder) cones or Strombolian types – these volcanoes erupted with fluid lava and less explosive material. Good examples are the Puys de Mercouer, Lassolas, Vache, Gouttes and Chopine. They account for 80 per cent of the volcanoes in the Puys chain.
- Domes or Pelean types – these produced thick lava which resulted in a strong explosion as viscous magma blocked the volcano's chimney and increased

Puy de Dôme from Walk 18

Extreme picnicking on Puy de Sancy

the build-up of pressure. Puy de Dôme is the best example of this type.

- Maars – these were hydromagnetic volcanoes in which magma and water reacted with each other, sending ash rocketing into the sky. The power of the explosion often resulted in a crater such as the case of Puy Pariou and Puy Nugere.

The Puys chain hosts the babies of the volcano world – eruptions took place 8,000–90,000 years ago. In contrast the Cantal supervolcano is the grandfather of the Auvergne volcanic family, having exploded 700,000–1 million years ago. The Sancy massif is in the middle, having been dormant for 25,000–300,000 years.

The volcanic ranges are rooted on a granite platform which came under pressure due to the thrust of the Alps and Pyrenees. Gassy magma got trapped in the cracks made by the tremendous pressure of this process and eventually the volcanoes blew their tops. Unerupted magma plugs formed the distinctive Châine des Puys (Monts Dômes) in the west of the region.

Auvergne's most famous volcanoes all feature on itineraries in this book. The 1465m Puy de Dôme has the distinction of being classified as a 'Grand Site de France'. Part of its renown stems from the fact that it is visible from all four *départements* of the region. The Cantal supervolcano – of which the Plomb du Cantal (1855m) is the highest point – is classed as the biggest volcano in Europe as it has a diameter bigger than Mount Etna. The massive volcanic edifice has been eroded by 12 glacial valleys that converge at the three main peaks of the Plomb, Puy Griou and the Puy Mary (1758m) which is also a Grand Site.

The main volcanic rock quarried in the Puys chain is pouzzolane. Its unique thermal and phonic qualities mean that it is useful for building due to its capacity to resist heat, filter water and get rid of odours. Trachyandesite is a silica-rich stone found in the Volvic area. It has been used in construction since the Middle Ages and is the distinctive rock used for the eye-catching cathedral at Clermont-Ferrand.

PLANTS AND WILDLIFE

At lower altitudes the predominant trees are beech, although oak, willow, alder and sweet chestnut will also be seen. The deciduous forest gives way to coniferous wood at higher altitudes, where pine dominates. Above the pine forests are moorland and sub-alpine zones. In the wetter west of the Auvergne pedunculate oaks are found mixed with beech, while on the drier granite slopes in the east the sessile oak is more common. Higher forests in the sub-montane zone tend to include European silver firs and mountain ash trees. Cow-wheat thrives in the beech forests and in higher woods the martagon lily, woodruff and Irish spurge flourish.

Meadow flowers near Domeyrat (Walk 33)

The most noticeable flowers are the yellow broom plants which give the lower mountain slopes and moors spectacular colour in early summer. Heather, sheep's bit and bilberry bushes are often nearby. Yellow gentians with their fleshy green leaves and towering stems are extremely widespread and adorn even the highest ridges of the Cantal and Sancy massifs. Blue gentians are also common at higher altitudes, along with ragwort, masterwort, bistort, saxifrage and wheatear. Among the less common flowers are Pyrenean squill, yellow wood anemone and alpine anemone.

Pearl bordered fritillary

The sheer number of butterflies fluttering about the Auvergne is astonishing. The region even boasts its own unique species, which is not difficult to spot, called the Auvergne Apollo. This is reputed to be the largest French butterfly and it lives exclusively in the Auvergne. The Apollo is white but has a red spot at the tip of its lower set of wings – and it has the uncanny knack of not sitting still for photographs. Other butterflies include the chequered blue, many different fritillaries and skippers. The peacock is very common, along with painted ladies and red admirals.

The authors can attest to the presence of wild boar in the Auvergne. These creatures are scarcely seen and are popular with hunters in the area (hunting wild boar is a favourite pastime of our Auvergnat neighbour). In the higher mountains there are small numbers of chamois and mouflon and even marmots, pine martens and

mountain goats. Badgers, roe deer, foxes, stoats and red deer can all be found at lower elevations. Otters and reputedly some beavers make the River Allier their home.

There are adders in the Auvergne region and walkers should be aware of what they look like in case the worst happens. They are recognisable due to a distinctive black pattern, similar to a chain of diamonds, running down their backs above lighter coloured flanks. Lizards are also common to the area. Atlantic salmon can be found in the Allier, but they are a protected species and fishing them is illegal. The Auvergne is perennially popular with fishermen. The rivers Loire and Allier are popular for carp fishing, whereas the Santoire and Alagnon in the Cantal are teeming with trout and grayling. The Senouire (Walks 29 and 33) has pike and there are perch and arctic char in the deep lakes such as Lake Pavin (Walk 24).

The Auvergne is also a bird watcher's paradise, with rare birds including the hoopoe, dwarf stern, squacco heron and the European bee-eater. The lower beech woods are home to tawny owls and jays. Skylarks and pipits frequent the moors and kestrels can often be spotted in the skies above the high meadows. In the mountainous areas bunting are common, along with nightjar, red-backed shrike, crag martins, redstarts, eagle owls and kites. Kingfishers and short-toed eagles can be found in the river gorges. The Chaudefour valley shelters

Horses with Puy de Peyre Arse and Puy Mary beyond

birds such as peregrine falcons, rock swallows and ravens. Woodpeckers are often heard tapping away in the peaceful Auvergne forests, as well as woodlarks and quail. Woodcocks and stock doves are less frequent sightings.

The volcanic *tourbières* (marshy volcanic crater lakes) have their own ecosystems. Plants include Scots pine, water clover, sun dew, downy willow, sedge, orchids and marsh cinquefoil. Frogs and coots love the peaty water while hen harriers can be seen in the skies above.

FOOD AND DRINK

Cheese

The Auvergne does nothing to dispel the cliché of the French population's excessive cheese-guzzling. The region is a hotbed of cheese-making and the cattle providing this traditional sustenance will inevitably be encountered roaming the hills on the walks included in this Guide. There are five celebrated cheeses of the Auvergne, which have each gained the coveted *Appellation Contrôlée* mark – a guarantee that a product can only be made in a very specific region. Cheese-lovers can easily combine visits to these dairy meccas with nearby walks.

Cantal is the oldest Auvergnat cheese and also the biggest seller, with nearly 14,800 tonnes of the stuff being churned each year. It varies from mild to extra-strong, and is a pressed hard cheese with a distinctive nutty taste made in huge 40kg blocks, using 400 litres of milk per block.

A Salers cow in the Cantal

Saint-Nectaire is the other best-seller, a soft cheese which is produced in farms and dairies around the town of the same name in the Puy de Dome *département*. It earned its name after the Marshal of France La Ferte-Sennecterre introduced the cheese to the court of the 'Sun King' Louis XIV.

Bleu d'Auvergne is produced across the region and originated with the brainwave of a 19th century farmer who decided to mix mouldy bread with milk. If that doesn't get your tastebuds tingling, rest assured that nowadays the powerful blue veins are produced by mixing the milk with *penicillium roqueforti* instead.

Fourme d'Ambert is a milder blue cheese made near Ambert in the Livradois Forez. According to legend it was popular with the Druids, who used it in rituals they performed in the Monts du Forez.

Salers comes from a town considered one of the most beautiful in France, which is found in the east of the Cantal département. This hard and pungent cheese can only be made for six months a year from the milk of cows exclusively fed on grass from volcanic mountains. It is aged for three months before getting to the *fromagerie*.

For those hungry for more there is a dedicated Cheese Route in the region with 36 mouthwatering stops on route (www.fromages-aop-auvergne.com).

Other Specialities

The Auvergne has a wealth of culinary resources, as well as excellent water filtered by volcanic rock. The Auvergne's vineyards are among the oldest in

21

France and the region produces one PDO (Protected Designation of Origin) wine called Saint-Pourcain as well as the respected Côtes d'Auvergne and Côtes Roannais. The cuisine is based around hearty staples and typical dishes are the potato based *truffade*, a hotpot called *la potée Auvergnat* and a kind of meatloaf with prunes called *pounti*. Delicious locally caught fish such as trout and char are also often served. The area – along with much of the rest of France – is not easy for strict vegetarians. Local beef is very prevalent – the hardworking cheesemaking Salers cattle also give top notch meat, which is a distinctive marbled bright red colour. Allier Charolais beef is even served up in the McDonalds restaurants around Clermont. The beef can be served cured, as mince, pâté, sausages or sautéed.

The main vegetable curiosity is the green Puy lentil, which heavily features on menus throughout the region. Interesting varieties of mushroom widely appear on your plate. A ubiquitous dessert dish is the bilberry tart, which is guaranteed to turn your mouth an enticing shade of blue. The Auvergne produces its own type of honey and local pastries and biscuits can be found in the numerous pâtisseries throughout the region.

Ever-present on the Auvergne hillsides, gentians are put to use in the regional aperitif called l'Avéze. Among its many medicinal claims, this alcoholic drink purports to be a digestive tonic, an antidepressant and a cure for fever. Gentian roots are also sold in rural shops as a base for herbal remedies.

Eating Out

Auvergne cuisine tends to be traditional simple peasant fare. Typically the *auberges* in rural regions offer a limited menu – perhaps three dishes and a reasonably priced *menu du jour*. This can be a three course meal and is usually less expensive at lunchtime than in the evening. Hungry walkers would do well to sample these menus as they are an easy way of getting acquainted with the local specialities. Outside the main cities expect to pay from €10–€20 for a menu du jour.

WHEN TO GO

The summer months are usually hot and sunny in the Auvergne, although the elevation of the Massif Central means that temperatures rarely become as sweltering as those in lower regions of southern France. Despite this, Clermont-Ferrand is reportedly one of the hottest cities in France. The region gets drier towards the east. Even in summer, temperatures drop quickly at night and evenings can often become chilly in the mountains. As evidenced by the smattering of ski resorts in the region, the Auvergne becomes a completely different proposition in the winter months, with snow covering the Cantal range and the Sancy massif throughout the

The Monts Dômes from Walk 25

season and intermittently affecting the higher territory in the Montagne Bourbonnaise and Haute-Loire areas as well. Many of the routes in this book would be extremely challenging in the winter months. Don't be put off visiting the region in the height of summer as many of the routes in the Guide take walkers through the beautiful verdant forests of the Auvergne, and some shady sections of hiking may well be appreciated on a sweltering August afternoon.

Massive temperature variations occur in the Cantal mountains and they retain snow in patches until summer. Also storms build very quickly and conditions change even more rapidly than in Britain. Visiting the Auvergne out of the traditional June–September season may bring a few frustrations – in the sleepier towns and villages some amenities do tend to be seasonal. Tourist information

offices and even restaurants cut down their opening hours in the spring and autumn months and buses can run less frequently.

GETTING THERE

Air

The most convenient airport is Clermont-Ferrand. Although this is an international airport, it has limited routes from outside France. At the time of writing Flybe has direct flights from Southampton to Clermont-Ferrand and is the best budget option. It also operates low cost connecting flights from Belfast, Leeds, Manchester, Edinburgh, Newcastle and Glasgow (www.flybe.com). From Heathrow Air France flies via Paris to Clermont-Ferrand (www.airfrance.co.uk). Many more operators fly direct from the UK to airports at Limoges (250km W of Clermont) and Lyon (220km E of Clermont). London City airport offers a flight to Brive-la-Gaillarde airport (140km W of Clermont) with www. citijet.com. These routes could be an option for those picking up a hire car.

Rail

Clermont-Ferrand is reached direct by high speed train from Paris Gare du Lyon in 3hr 30min. Vichy can be reached direct in slightly less time. It is simple to book a connecting 2hr Eurostar train journey from St Pancras to Paris through the SNCF website (www.sncf.co.uk) although ample time to change stations in Paris should be allowed.

Road

Taking your own car to France from the UK is simple. Many companies operate cross channel car ferries. Norfolk Lines (www.norfolkline.com) is a good budget option, whereas P&O (www.poferries.com) and Sea France (www.seafrance.com) have crossings at all times of day. Another speedy option is to go through the Eurotunnel from Folkestone with your car (www.eurotunnel.com).

From Calais it is nearly 700km to Clermont-Ferrand and it takes roughly 7hrs to drive using the excellent *autoroutes*. The one downside of the French *autoroutes* is the cost. One way from Calais to the Auvergne will cost €25–30.

GETTING AROUND

Many of the routes detailed in this book are accessible by public transport but bear in mind that in some

The picturesque village of Allègre

areas buses only run twice a day and it can be difficult to plan walking around the timetables. Useful websites for planning walks around the local bus network are: www.puydedome.fr, www.cantal.fr, www.hauteloire.fr and www.allier.fr (see the 'Public Transport' information at the start of each route). The local rail network (TER) is fairly good and cheap in comparison with the UK. Major towns such as Puy-en-Velay and Vichy are well served by rail. Useful for routes in this book are the stations at Murat, Lioran, Mont-Dore, Volvic and Brioude. Find information on times and services at www.ter-sncf.com/Regions/auvergne/fr/. Where routes are accessible by bus or train we have stated this in the information box that precedes the route descriptions. Bigger villages do have taxi services but these can be expensive and difficult to arrange. Hitchhiking is perfectly possible, even common, particularly in rural areas.

ACCOMMODATION

The wide variety of accommodation on offer in rural France can be baffling but can also be a highlight of your visit. Traditional hotels are found in larger towns, whereas smaller Auvergne villages generally have an *auberge* or 'inn'. These often have plenty of character and tend to serve limited menus based on local produce.

Most larger villages have a campsite and these are generally of good quality. In all but the most touristy destinations campsites are open from May–September. Municipal campsites tend to be good value for money and are often in great spots close to village centres, although numerous private campsites exist offering varying degrees of luxury.

The same rules apply to the ubiquitous *gîtes*, which can be anything from bunkhouses to sumptuous villas. *Gîtes* are generally privately owned cottages that provide self-catering accommodation for 2–12 people and can be booked year round for a week or weekend. There are thousands of these across the Auvergne in delightful locations. A good starting point is the Gîtes de France website en.gites-de-france.com, which is in English. *Gîtes d'étape* are specifically designed for hikers and cyclists. They are often in remote mountainous locations and function like refuges. These can be booked at www.gites-refuges.com, where there is an option to translate the website.

Chambres d'hôtes are also plentiful across the region. These are similar to B&Bs, although it is best to check whether breakfast is included. They are generally rooms in the owner's property and sometimes traditional evening meals are available. For those touring the Auvergne by motorhome there are many *Aires de Services* (motorhome stops) and *Aires de Stationnement* (parking areas) which are often free of charge. The websites www.i-campingcar.fr and www.

campingcar-infos.com list these. The following information should give you a basic idea of different options and bases in the five main walking areas of the Auvergne (see 'Using this Guide' below) but it is by no means comprehensive.

Cantal

Murat (Walk 5) is a small medieval town with good facilities which acts as a gateway to the mountains and makes a sensible base for exploring the region. Options include a good municipal campsite www.camping-murat.com. There are several gîtes. Contact Jean-Pierre Seccaud on 04 7120 1187 or Martine Nairabeze on 04 7120 0080 www.legitedemartine.fr. For chambres d'hôtes La Gaspardine is 04 7120 0191 or Grange de la Bastide on 04 7120 2414. The Les Messageries hotel www.hotel-les-messageries.com is central and the Hotel aux Globetrotters is another option on 04 7120 0722. The tourist information office in the main square is very helpful and will book accommodation in the area for you. The Gîtes de France website www.gites-de-france.com can be used to book the mountain refuges in the Cantal including some of the *burons* (cheese-making barns) which function as gîtes d'étapes.

The ski resort of Lioran is another base and has a plethora of hotel choices. These cater for winter skiers and can do good summer deals. The Les Sources gîte is on 04 7147

0533. Other Cantal villages with campsites include St Jacques des Blats www.camping-des-blats.fr, Camping du Laveisierre 04 7120 1134 and Camping d'Albepierre 04 7120 0280. *Gîtes* and auberges are plentiful in the region and almost every significant village in the Cantal has accommodation of some sort. The gîtes and auberge near to Les Gardes (Walk 3) would prove a very quiet spot. Mandailles (Walk 13) is a very well positioned central village from which all walks in the Cantal are easily accessed, it has gîtes and an auberge. Mandailles also has a campsite just north of the village, but at the time of writing this inexplicably only opened in absolute peak season.

Châine des Puys (Monts Dômes) and Monts Dore

The large village of Orcival (Walk 18) has many good restaurant choices and is ideally situated between the two mini-ranges of the Châine des Puys and the Monts Dore. All the walks in both sections can quickly be accessed from it by car. Good hotel options are the Notre Dame www.hotelnotredame-orcival.com or Hotel des Touristes 04 7365 8255. The gîte d'étape Du Pont is on 04 7365 9405.

The smaller nearby village of St Bonnet pres Orcival (Walk 18) is also a great place to base yourself and much quieter. There is an excellent campsite there on 04 7365 8332 which also rents chalets. The Panda gîte at St Bonnet is on 04 7365 8791 and Les Chalets de la Haute Sioule on 04 7365 8332. Chambres d'hôtes can be booked at www.vareilles-nature. com.

Another option is to stay in the busier small spa town of Mont-Dore (Walks 22 and 23) where there are plenty of hotels although many come with a high price tag and it is a longer drive to the Châine des Puys from there. Mont-Dore is a good choice of base for those travelling by public transport as it has a railway station, and several walks are accessible from the town. Mont-Dore has some gîte options that can double as chalets in the winter. The Maison des Longes is well located, www.maisondeslonges.com. There are also several campsites including La Plage Verte www.plage-verte.com and Camping Grande Cascade www. camping-grandecascade.com.

Haute-Loire

Allègre (Walks 31 and 32) is a small but pleasant base with choices such as a lovely municipal campsite www. mairie-allegre.com, a hotel restaurant www.hotel-leydier43.com, luxury gîtes at www.domaine-de-fonteline. com, gîtes d'étape on 04 7100 7688 and chambres d'hôtes at www. lemoulinpicard.fr. For those wishing to stop overnight at Chaise-Dieu (Walk 29) there are two gîtes d'étape: La Penide 04 7100 0676 and Le Close d'Âtre 04 7100 0173; and several hotels including La Casadei www. hotel-la-casadei.com. Lavaudieu (Walk 35) has two chambres d'hôtes on 04 7176 4504 and 04 7176 4902.

In Le Puy-en-Velay innumerable chain and independent hotel options exist and are best searched for on a hotel or travel site such as www. expedia.com, www.tripadvisor.com or www.booking.com. Hotel des

The unique cityscape of Le Puy en Velay

Capucins offers apartments and gîtes: www.lescapucins.net. Gîte d'étape Maison Saint-François is on 04 7105 9886 and the large campsite at Brives Charensac 4km outside the city is at www.camping-audinet.fr.

Montagne Bourbonnaise
There is a good choice of accommodation in areas near the walks, including a wealth of gîtes – there is no room for an exhaustive list here. Mayet de Montagne is a good base which offers a decent range of accommodation and facilities including a supermarket. Hotel choices include La Vieille Auberge 04 7059 3401, La Magnette 04 7059 7524, Printemps 04 7059 7124 or Le Relais du Lac 04 7059 7023. Chambres d'hôtes can be booked at www.le-couturon.com. There is also a nice municipal campsite and a more luxurious one at Les Plans in nearby St Clement www.vacances-lesplans.com. Campervans can also park overnight in a designated area in the village centre.

The quaint village of Ferriéres sur Sichon (Walks 36 and 37) is another good choice of base. The Auberge du Sichon 04 7041 1006 in the village centre serves quality regional fare, chambres d'hôtes are available on 04 7045 1737 and the tranquil municipal campsite is by an attractive river and lake. Both Mayet and Ferriéres have helpful tourist information offices and a good number of gîtes are available to rent.

Further north St Nicolas (Walks 41 and 42) has a pleasant campsite Les Myrtilles 04 7056 4003, gîte La Bourbonnière 04 7056 4099, chambres d'hôtes www.montagnedor.nl and a hotel restaurant Bold'air 04 7056 4150. In the picturesque hilltop village of Châtel Montagne (Walk 38) the best option is the Camping de la Croix Cognat 04 7059 3138 or chambres d'hôtes and gîtes are available by calling 04 7059 3670. If you want to spend time in the spa town of Vichy www.ville-vichy.fr lists plentiful accommodation options there.

DIFFICULTY

The walks in this Guide have been divided into three broad levels of difficulty.
- Grade 1. On easy tracks and broad paths. Reasonably short walks with few navigational problems, little height gain and generally gentle terrain.
- Grade 2. Walks that will not be taxing for a fit and experienced hiker. These may contain occasional navigational difficulties and involve a longer route and some steep terrain and moderate height gain.
- Grade 3. Challenging walks designed for hikers experienced in the British hills. Steep, rocky terrain may be encountered and considerable ascents may be made involving longer days in the mountains.

Runners pass the Col de Cabre on the Puy de Peyre Arse horseshoe – travelling light!

EQUIPMENT

Only standard hiking equipment is necessary for all walks in this book from May to October. High factor **suncream** is essential, especially on the high mountains where the altitude magnifies the sun-burn risk. It should be carried even on apparently heavy grey days as clouds disperse rapidly in the Auvergne. A good pair of **hiking boots** is recommended for Grade 2 and 3 routes. Grade 1 walks can be easily accomplished in trainers. A warm **sweater** or **fleece**, light **waterproof jacket** and **hat** should be carried on long mountain routes as weather can change quickly. Shorts are not advised on many routes in the Montagne Bourbonnaise and Haute-Loire during May and June due to the risk of ticks in this season (see

'Hazards and Emergencies') and light **trousers** will prove preferable.

Carry plenty of **water** as it is easy to become dehydrated on long hot days; a litre per person should suffice, even on the longest routes in this book. Take care not to wear too many layers as overheating will make you require more water.

'Light is right!' Something the authors have noted in recent years is a growing trend for British hikers to carry a ridiculous amount of unnecessary gear, throwing everything including the kitchen sink into stupidly large rucksacks. Ask yourself before setting off, 'do I really need this?'. Remember, lugging unnecessary weight around will hinder the enjoyment of your hiking, slow you down and tire you out. Always pack a **map** and a **compass**.

Mobile phones are useful but do not rely on getting a signal. If setting off later in the day a **headtorch** might be a worthwhile precaution.

MAPS

For all but the Grade 1 walks in this guide a map is recommended. Detailed topographical maps are available for all the areas covered. A Series Bleu IGN map at 1:25,000 incorporates the entire Cantal section, two cover the Châine des Puys and Massif du Sancy. The Montagne Bourbonnaise walks are mainly covered by the Mayet-de-Montagne map and the Haute-Loire by the Allegre/La Chaise Dieu maps. The full names of the IGN 1:25,000 sheets, if you are ordering online or by phone, are shown below.

Each map is widely sold in the area which it covers but unlike in Britain it can be infuriating getting them elsewhere: you may, for example, encounter problems getting hold of a map of the Cantal from shops in the Monts Dore, despite being so nearby. Indeed, the authors spent an entire afternoon and failed to find a single shop selling maps of the Monts Dore in the major town of Vichy. Supermarkets, hypermarkets and bookshops are usually a good bet for stocking maps of the wider region, but there are no guarantees. Tourist information offices and newsagents usually sell IGN maps of their near area. The IGN maps are available prior to departure in the UK from Amazon, Stamfords, the Map Shop and other good retailers on and offline.

A word of caution about the IGN maps of this region. Partially due to the lack of a rights of way system which we have in Britain, but also clearly as a result of some lazy mapping, some of the tracks and paths appearing on the 1:25,000 maps in the Auvergne do not exist on the ground. They have probably fallen into disuse, but in some instances we have found 'disuse' to equate to decades of absence. Similarly, many other

1 The Cantal	2435OT Monts du Cantal
2 The Châine des Puys (Monts Dômes)	2531ET Châine des Puys
3 The Monts Dore	2432ET Massif du Sancy
4 The Haute-Loire: Forez and Velay	2734O Allègre/La Chaise Dieu 2735E Le Puy en Velay 2634E Paulhaguet 2634O Brioude
5 The Montagne Bourbonnaise	2730O Mayet de Montagne 2729O Lapalisse 2730E St Just/Monts de la Madeleine

A confusing array of signage

Way of St James signs in the Cantal

good and long-established paths on the ground are not marked at all on the maps. Added to this, the distinction between paved roads and tracks is often not made. We have tried to clear up this issue and others in our route descriptions.

WAYMARKING

Many sections of routes in this book are waymarked. This can be a succession of coloured stripes painted onto rocks or trees or small plaques stuck onto gates or buildings. There are also occasional arrows and signs to forthcoming villages and landmarks. Grand Randonnée (GR) routes are usually waymarked in red and white whereas Petit Randonees (PR) vary between green, yellow, blue and red. Other associations involved in waymarking

such as Chamina and local authorities can use other symbols. These can get both colourful and confusing in areas where many paths exist and are rarely consistent enough to provide a good substitute for a map. Of course many paths and tracks without any waymarking are equally good. Access is generally permitted unless signs tell you otherwise. If in doubt, consult this guide and a map. Coloured crosses at the start of paths and tracks simply mean a route off the waymarked hike, many of which are taken by our routes: they do not bar the way.

HAZARDS AND EMERGENCIES

The general emergency number in France is 112.

Cows and often horses freely roam on high pastures along many of

A formidable bull on a Cantal farm

the routes in this book. The authors have had little trouble with these but it is best to give any calves or foals a wide berth and not to pass through herds. The best policy if large animals do get too close is to make firm large movements with your arms or sticks and raise your voice in low tones.

The management of dairy cattle in the Auvergne, especially in the cheese mecca of the Cantal, means barriers and obstacles change position regularly. Hikers are given far more responsibility and expected to employ far greater initiative when negotiating fences in the region than those accustomed to hiking in Britain will be used to. Single line electric fences can be found on some of the paths, particularly in the Cantal. Although these can

be perturbing when first encountered, they are genuinely there to stop cattle and not hikers. Where paths cross electric fences there is usually some obvious means of either opening or passing through them. This can be a plastic hook handle on the wire or you may be simply expected to duck underneath. If the latter option is taken, be sure to remove any rucksacks from your back! The same scenario is played out when negotiating barbed wire fences. Some have flexible gates but these can prove far more awkward to operate than simply ducking underneath.

It is not advisable to drink any **water from streams** in the Auvergne, no matter what the altitude. This is due to possible pollution from the extensive cattle grazing which takes place even on the highest slopes and at quite extraordinary altitudes in the Monts Dore and Cantal. There are many springs or *sources d'eau* marked on the IGN maps and the water from these tends to be extremely pure – this is the region of Volvic after all – and these are less likely to suffer from pollution by livestock. For those wild camping, water purification tablets and boiling water first are essential.

The forests and meadows of the Auvergne can be a haven for **ticks**, particularly in the damper spring months. Ticks lie in the undergrowth waiting for an unsuspecting creature or hiker to pass by. You cannot feel them attach themselves but it is suggested you check your legs after walking in the region as ticks must be removed quickly to prevent the risk of infection. A pair of tweezers and a twisting motion does this job easily. However, keep an eye on the affected area or areas and should a red ring appear on your leg as much as a week after a suspected tick bite, seek medical assistance immediately, as this may be a sign of Lyme disease.

The **farm dogs** prevalent in hamlets throughout rural Auvergne often make a racket but are usually tethered.

USING THIS GUIDE

The Auvergne is a huge region and to cover its walking fully would require a mammoth tome. Therefore this guide focuses on five areas where there is significant walking territory within reach of a convenient base. Two or more of these areas might reasonably be explored on a two-week holiday and the best of the region's hiking can easily be discovered by doing this.

For each walk, a sketch map and detailed route description is provided, along with basic information relevant to the route (distance, ascent, difficulty (graded 1 to 3, see 'Difficulty' above), approximate timing, IGN map and details of parking and public transport links), as well as incidental points of interest along the route.

The superb Cantal range would be the first port of call for those seeking high mountain adventure. The compact geography of the massif – formed by one supervolcano – would lend itself to an energetic week exploring its major summits from a base such as the attractive town of Murat.

Rivalling the Cantal for its unique landscape and scarred by intense volcanic activity are the Chaîne des Puys and Monts Dore ranges. These are two separate mini areas but run into each other and both can be easily accessed from a base such as Orcival. The Chaîne des Puys (also known as the Monts Dômes) is perfect for shorter hill walks as there are no real elongated ridges and multi-peak link ups. The Monts Dore centre on the Massif de Sancy (at 1885m the highest peak in the Auvergne) and lend themselves to mountainous circuits; but we have

Beside the Senouire at Lavaudieu (photo: Jean Pol Grandmont)

also found room for some less strenuous itineraries.

The Haute-Loire is a vast area so we have chosen to concentrate on the southern part of the department, which gives a contrast to the preceding chapters. The walks focus on the historic area of the Velay and exploring the Parc de Livradois Forez.

All the walking in this section can be accessed from the unmissable fairy-tale city of Le Puy en Velay.

The final chapter focuses on the most enticing part of the northeastern Auvergne department of Allier, where the pastoral Montagne Bourbonnaise can be found. This is a compact and beautiful unspoilt walking area.

THE CANTAL

The path to Roc d'Hoziéres (Walk 12)

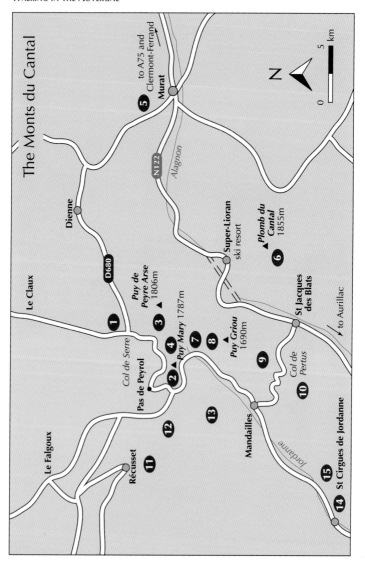

The Monts du Cantal

to A75 and
Clermont-Ferrand

Murat

5

N122

Alagnon

Dienne

D680

Super-Lioran
ski resort

*Plomb du
Cantal*
1855m ▲

6

Le Claux

*Puy de
Peyre Arse*
1806m ▲

3

Puy Mary 1787m

1

St Jacques
des Blats

to Aurillac

Col de Serre

4

7

8

Puy Griou
1690m ▲

Pas de Peyrol

2

9

Col de
Pertus

Le Falgoux

12

13

10

Mandailles

Jordanne

11

Récusset

St Cirgues de Jordanne

15

14

N

0   5   km

INTRODUCTION

Formed by Europe's largest known supervolcano, the Monts du Cantal offer hikers a spectacular array of walks amid some of the finest scenery in France. In many ways the Cantal is the French answer to the English Lake District – only without the actual lakes.

It is the cheesemaking heartland of the Auvergne, with the region's *route des fromages* focussed in the area and herds of curly-horned cattle to be found grazing on lofty ridge top pastures alongside colourful clusters of gentians. Conveniently confined to a single 1:25,000 map, the Cantal mountains provide a superb concentration of easily accessed walks to suit the full spectrum of hiking ability.

The peaks themselves tend to be dramatic and steep, yet also inviting, as summits from which to gaze wondrously while munching baguettes are relatively easily attained. This is partly because of a road network which crosses four major cols, the most famous of these being the perennial Tour de France favourite, the Pas de Peyrol (1588m). The Cantal massif forms the most southerly extension of the Parc des Volcans and the extinct supervolcano has left behind a number of great conical peaks, including the famous Grand Site of France Puy Mary (1787m), Puy de Peyre Arse (1806m), Griou (1690m) and the Auvergne's second highest peak, the Plomb du Cantal (1855).

The Cantal is one of the most sparsely populated départements in France, with the only major city being Aurillac in the south. The Cantal massif has harsh winters and summer storms are also common. The most impressive terrain is concentrated in an area bisected by the N122 road so it makes sense to use the historic town of Murat as a base. Murat was the scene of Resistance fighting and harsh reprisals during the German Occupation in World War II. As well as having a charming medieval town centre and easy access to the mountains, Murat boasts good facilities which include a supermarket, cinema, tourist office and good restaurants. The town has accommodation to suit every budget from campsites and chambres d'hôtes to gîtes and hotels.

Another choice of base which may offer good value for money in summer months is the purpose-built ski resort of Lioran. Other beautiful Cantal villages and hamlets such as Laveissiére, St Cirgues de Jordanne, St Jacques des Blats and the perfectly situated Mandailles provide self-catering and camping options for those wanting to stay further off the beaten track.

WALK 1
Puy de Niermont

Start/Finish	Col de Serre
Distance	8km
Total Ascent	350m
Difficulty	2
Time	2hrs 45mins
Highest Point	1620m
Map	IGN 1:25,000 Sheet 2435OT *Monts du Cantal*
Parking	Car park near junction of D62 and D680 Pas de Peyrol road

The summit of Puy de Niermont offers walkers outstanding views of almost all the major peaks in the Cantal, from the Plomb du Cantal and Griou in the east, the Puy de Peyre Arse and Puy Mary in the centre, to the distant Puy Violent in the southwest: a platform from which to be introduced to the layout of the Cantal could not have been better designed nor situated. Easily accessed from the Pas de Peyrol road, being of average length with little difficulty and in an outstanding location, this route up Niermont is a particularly good starting point for the Monts du Cantal.

The walk provides a round trip: the outbound section is less frequented and saves the best of views for the return leg, where the terrain is moderate enough to ensure the delightful panorama ahead can be fully savoured.

Follow the main path NE out of the **car park** for 250m, passing through two gates. At the second gate turn left, leading onto a wide grassy track which stays level, heading into the mixed deciduous forests underneath the ridge top.

Continue along the pleasant forest track for 1.5km, gaining little height until a short rise. At the brow of a small hill **two tracks** come off left – one descending to Le Claux and another towards the hamlet of La Peyre Grosse. Ignore these and take a right hand track ascending through a gate. This becomes a grassy path shortly after the gate and commences the main part of the climb

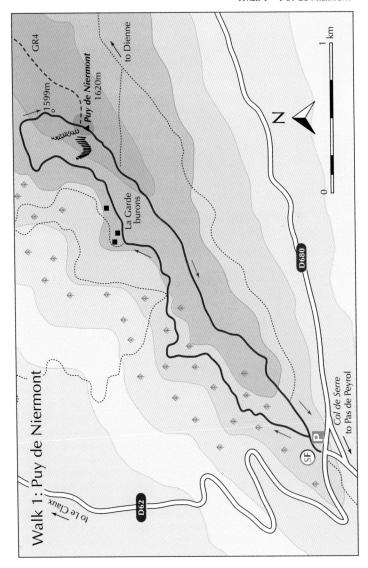

Walk 1: Puy de Niermont

GR4

1599m

Puy de Niermont
1620m

to Dienne

La Garde
burons

N

1 km

0

D680

D62

to Le Claux

SF

Col de Serre
to Pas de Peyrol

P

Le Garde burons on Puy de Niermont

to Puy de Niermont, bending steeply rightwards and is marked with red posts.

After 100m of steep hiking the path relents. Leave the red posts behind and, following a green waymarker, trend leftwards. The route now contours to a promontory at the head of the small **Abri valley** where the **La Garde** *burons* (or barns for cheese-making) can be found. At the highest of these ruins, a good traverse path is picked up which aims for the distinctive grey scree slope below the now visible summit of Puy de Niermont.

As the path continues hikers will see another set of ruins beneath them to the left and views of the Limon plateau and the Monts Dore open up ahead. The path is bumpy in parts but is easy to follow. It traverses the hillside above the treeline but just below the scree slope. After 200m the path bypasses a buttress of rock and soon meets a barbed wire fence which must be dipped under – do not be concerned that you are off route, hikers are expected to employ such tactics in the Cantal, only remember to remove your rucksack before ducking under the fence!

The path continues to contour around the hillside, gradually gaining the wide summit ridge at Niermont's rear (do not be tempted to cut off the corner and head more directly to the summit). Pass easily across another fence and trend right-wards (S) to join a grassy track. Two summits are visible here – the right hand of the two is the peak of **Puy de Niermont** and is marked with a metal post, a wind direction funnel, a granite pillar and **small rocky outcrops**.

> Here you can feast your eyes upon the full splendour of the **Monts du Cantal panorama**. The immediate peak is the Puy de Peyre Arse with its snaking north ridge separating the Impredine and Santoire valleys. Beyond this, the triangular fin of the Puy Griou rears its head. The pyramidical peak to the right is the famous Puy Mary, a popular French emblem.

Leave the summit, heading S on a path passing immediately under a barbed wire fence. The ridge top path is now well worn and easy to follow to the right of another fence. For the most part it is gently inclined and allows you ample time to soak up the views. Only a steep rocky section after 200m will give pause for thought: this is negotiated by a series of switchbacks. Due to erosion the path goes left and care must be taken on the loose ground here.

Shortly after this steepening, a marked path to **Dienne** descends to the left. Ignore this and continue straight ahead across a saddle where cows often congregate. Pleasurable walking on mainly good grassy terrain with superb views takes you back down to the car park at the **Col de Serre**.

WALK 2
An Ascent of the Puy de Peyre Arse

Start/Finish	La Gravière
Distance	14.5km
Total Ascent	1050m
Difficulty	3
Time	5–6hrs (4hrs if using escape route)
Highest Point	1806m
Map	IGN 1:25,000 Sheet 2435OT *Monts du Cantal*
Public Transport	Train to Murat and taxi
Parking	Parking area at N end of La Gravière

With its airy ridges, rocky outcrops and pristine glacial valleys, Puy de Peyre Arse is one of the most attractive hiking destinations in the Cantal, as well its second highest summit. Giving similar difficulties to a challenging Lakeland horseshoe, the hike offers breathtaking views of the entire range, including the Puys Mary and Griou and the Plomb du Cantal. Heather, broom and mountain flowers flourish on these lofty slopes, along with an unlikely collection of daffodils for those visiting in spring or early summer. The ridge walk also takes in the aptly named Téton (breast) de Vénus. An authors' favourite, this route is strongly recommended for seasoned hikers.

Access is from the parking area at the north end of the small village of **La Gravière**, where there are some benches by a river and a drinking water point. From here head up the middle of three lanes into the village, following a sign for Le Boudin. After 60m there is a crossroads with a horse trough fountain. Head straight uphill towards the prominent cross on top of the distinctive nearby cliffs. ◄

Looking S up the Santoire valley the distinctive Téton de Vénus and dramatic crags of Puy Bataillouse are visible.

Head steeply up the narrow road to the hamlet of **La Courbatière**. Here take the road up right until reaching a sign for Col de Serre. Follow this for only 50m, then take a pleasant grassy path branching off left uphill, leaving the Col de Serre path. This now swings round beneath the cliffs with the cross which overlook the village.

Passing over a shoulder to the right of the cliffs the crags of Puy de la Tourte emerge in the distance to the W. Go past a stream which feeds two water troughs and do not be perturbed by a barbed wire fence at **1258m**, under which you must dip. This is at the bottom of a wood where a makeshift sign points right to the 'Peyre Arse'. Ignore this and follow a better track left (N) uphill, initially heading back towards the cliffs.

After a couple of switchbacks you will find yourself deposited on the broad spine of the Peyre Arse ridge crest. ▶ Head on past the extensive Peyre Arse **buron ruins**, veering left above them but always aiming to return to the ridge crest proper.

You may encounter horses roaming here.

The path becomes more pronounced as the ridge narrows and the distant summit of Peyre Arse emerges, as does the col between it and Bataillouse; the alluring Téton de Vénus and the dangerous-looking shark fin of Puy Griou in the further distance can also be appreciated.

Imposing **crags at 1598m** appear initially to bar the way but the path negotiates these with little difficulty. You are soon drawn to a wonderful humpback. Stay on the absolute crest as it leads over the 1707m and 1747m spot heights, ignoring any temptation to traverse beneath the humpback as an easy clamber

Sculpture at La Graviére

43

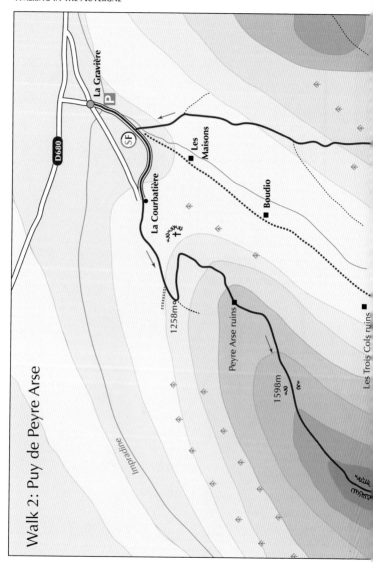

Walk 2: Puy de Peyre Arse

La Gravière

D680

P

SF

Les Maisons

La Courbatière

Boudio

1258m

Peyre Arse ruins

1598m

Les Trois Cols ruins

Impradine

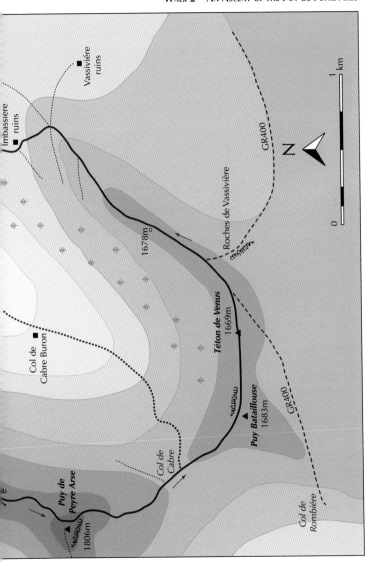

up a small rock step will bring you to a superb heathery path which negotiates this airy feature. The descent from the humpback appears steep but is negotiated steadily enough by following the zigzags down to the narrow col at 1706m. From here you will head steeply up to the summit of **Peyre Arse**, which is modestly marked by a small granite pillar and has spectacular views.

Leave the summit initially by retracing your steps for 100m until a clear path right (SE) can be taken down through the heather, skirting beneath crags and down to the **Col de Cabre**.

> At the Col de Cabre an **escape path** leads NE from the horseshoe straight back down to La Gravière if you've had enough. Take the obvious steep PR path down past a large boulder on the right. This becomes a walled marked path then turns into a track at the Col de Cabre buron and eventually a road at Boudio.

But the hardest hiking is over and most will have plenty of enthusiasm left to complete the horseshoe. Take the faint grassy path SE. This becomes more established for a steep section up to **Puy Bataillouse**. Go through a small wire fence, following wooden posts along the ridge and being wary of the splendid cliffs to the left. The climb onwards to the Téton is well worth the extra effort for those who have continued.

From the summit of the **Téton de Venus** retrace your steps for 10m and pick up the path down to a gate meeting the GR400 route. Do not take this but follow the leftmost line of bleached fence posts, where an unlikely but good path soon establishes itself, and continue to ascend to the left of the posts. The final high point of **1678m** is marked by a cairn and the picturesque Puy de Seycheuse (1650m) appears ahead.

Continue on the path, following the posts down to the col where you will see the **Imbassibière ruins** to the left. Head down to these. The path momentarily disappears here. Simply follow the watercourse straight down

The striking line of bleached wooden posts on the Peyre Arse horseshoe

for 80m until a N-trending wide grassy path appears – take this. It becomes more rocky and briefly dips through some trees. At a junction with a farm track and a stream turn right. With care pass through a first barbed wire fence – this can be opened but proves awkward. ▶ A second barbed wire fence is easily stepped over by a natural stile.

At a fork take the left way and note that in spring you may have to contend with an inconvenient stream running down the track as well as some awkward bouldery terrain. Ignore a final track branching left and continue towards the village. At the time of writing there was a final obstacle of a one wire electric cattle fence just before **La Gravière**. ▶

The fence is there to prohibit the widely seen cows, not hikers.

Such fences are not permanent fixtures. Hikers are expected to negotiate them crawling under them – they do things differently in France.

WALK 3

*Puy Mary with optional excursion to
Puy de la Tourte*

Start/Finish	Pas de Peyrol parking area on the D680
Distance	2.5km (plus 4km for Puy de la Tourte)
Total Ascent	200m (plus 120m for Puy de la Torte)
Difficulty	1 (2 with Puy de la Tourte)
Time	50mins (plus 1½hrs for Puy de la Tourte)
Highest Point	1783m
Map	IGN 1:25,000 Sheet 2435OT *Monts du Cantal*

On a sunny afternoon the Pas de Peyrol swarms with tourists visiting one of France's 37 designated Grand Sites and masochistic lycra-clad cyclists pitting themselves against the steep switchbacks of the pass. Visit in the early morning or towards dusk, however, and the area is far more tranquil, and swarming only with swifts and the occasional paraglider.

More than 500,000 people visit the Grand Site of Puy Mary each year, and because of these huge numbers a slightly unsightly concrete path up the peak from the pass has been installed to curb erosion. In our view this path is best either tackled outside peak hours or followed up with an extension to the rarely frequented summit of Puy de la Tourte, from where the stream of people ascending Puy Mary can be observed. The Pas de Peyrol has a tourist information office, a trinket shop, public toilets and a café.

The road up the Pas de Peyrol, with an average gradient of 12 per cent over the final 3km, has proved a popular place for watching professional cyclists show their mettle in the Tour de France.

◀ From the S side of the **pass**, follow the wide concrete path snaking up the ridge to the summit of **Puy Mary** in a leisurely 25 minutes. There is no scope for going off course here. The summit provides excellent views and an orientation table. Most tourists will return to the pass by retracing their steps. A better way is to continue SE from the summit.

The route down the back of Puy Mary is the opposite of the concrete steps, providing quite exposed hiking, passing through a rocky fin and down a small steep step. On descending take care on the wooden sleepers which can rock. After about 500m look out for a grassy path

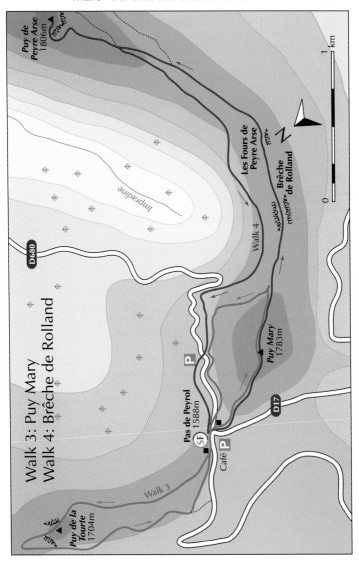

Walk 3: Puy Mary
Walk 4: Brêche de Rolland

Puy de Peyre Arse 1806m

Les Fours de Peyre Arse

Brêche de Rolland

Impradine

D680

Walk 4

Puy Mary 1783m

Pas de Peyrol 1588m

SF

Café P

P

D17

Walk 3

Puy de la Tourte 1704m

N

0   1 km

Puy Mary's north east face holding snow from Puy de la Tourte

Those wishing to elongate their Puy Mary excursion, could consider a traverse of the Brêche de Rolland – see Walk 4.

which strikes off left and leads round the NE side of the mountain. Follow this traversing path round the peak and join the road for the last 100m to the pass. ◄

Extension to Puy de la Tourte

A satisfying way to spend the afternoon is to ascend Puy Mary and then take a break perhaps in the **café** at the top of the pass. After recouping some energy, the discerning hiker may notice a further enticing objective overlooking the N side of the pass. This is Puy de la Tourte, and a hike along the ridge to its summit gives an enjoyable outing in itself without the crowds and with stunning views of the earlier route to Puy Mary.

Set off from **Pas de Peyrol** on the obvious path up the ridge. After 200m the GR route leaves this path. Stay on the right hand side of the peak until the ridge top is joined to give stunning hiking and superb views of the Mars valley and the Puy Violent to the W. Make a short traverse right of the crags and follow the path to the **summit**, which is marked by a cairn. Continue on the path over the top of the summit. About 5m after passing a metal post turn to your right and head down the grass to find a clear well-worn path. (If you find yourself above

any **rocks** do not descend). Initially the path heads back towards Puy Mary but after 20m turns left and negotiates the rocky buttresses of Tourte's summit. It is the only safe way down this side of the mountain. Pass under the **summit rocks** and continue to descend quite steeply below the main ridge crest. Cross a barbed wire fence at its lowest point and follow the path on its left side until the larger GR path is visible. Cut across to this and take it leftwards, ascending gradually at first, then contouring round after crossing a fence. ▶ When the path splits, stay with the higher option and follow this all the way back to the **Pas de Peyrol**.

Puy de la Tourte from Puy Mary

Excellent views of the Chavaroche and the white dome of the Roc d'Hoziéres unfurl.

WALK 4

Traverse of the Brêche de Rolland from Puy Mary to Peyre Arse

Start/Finish	Pas de Peyrol parking area on the D680
Distance	9km
Total Ascent	580m
Difficulty	3
Time	3hrs 30mins (shorter alternative route 2hrs 30mins)
Highest Point	1806m (shorter alternative route 1685m)
Map	IGN 1:25,000 Sheet 2435OT *Monts du Cantal*

The Brêche ('break') de Rolland is a distinctive steep-sided notch in the snaking ridge which connects the Puy Mary to the Puy de Peyre Arse and truly provides a superb wander through the heart of the Cantal massif. While the full circuit includes both of those major summits, for hikers who have previously conquered them and do not wish to retrace their steps, the delights of the Brêche can still be sampled by following Option B and simply omitting one or both peaks.

See map for Walk 3

Leave the **Pas de Peyrol** parking area on the signposted Puy Mary path between the tourist information and toilet buildings. From here head up the concrete steps to the summit of **Puy Mary**. At the summit of Puy Mary continue straight ahead down steep rocky terrain to the point on the SE section of the mountain where a path joins from the left.

Continue straight ahead along a clear ridge path augmented by occasional wooden sleepers. A steep rocky natural staircase leads to the break of the **Brêche de Rolland**. Initially this appears forbiddingly steep, but proves a very easy scramble overcome by thousands of hikers each year. Care must be taken here however, especially in wet weather. The rock is sound and handholds and convenient steps abound. ◀ Having negotiated the winding staircase of rock into the break, you will soon find yourself clambering out of it, up wooden sleepers. The path now continues without any difficulty passing

If in doubt or apprehensive, face into the rock as this is a more secure means of descent.

over **les Fours de Peyre Arse** before travelling a further 1km along the ridge to where there is a clear meeting of paths.

Ignore the descending path going rightwards towards the Col de Cabre, which is marked with a red and white line. Note the leftwards descending path from here which will be taken later. Instead follow the path up the ridge, marked with green and red crosses, passing a large cairn after 100m.

Approach the forbidding summit rocks of Peyre Arse and stay on the main path just left of an outcrop where an easy rocky step gains access to the summit area avoiding the worst of the crags. This provides a circuitous but safe way to the **summit** (if you are scrambling, you are off route). ▶

From the summit retrace your steps for 1km and look out for a gap in the fence which gives access to the already noted path which now forks to your right. This runs roughly parallel to the outbound route, but traverses beneath the fine north facing crags of the Brèche rather than on top of them. The **D680** road is eventually met at a hairpin bend. Head through the gate and after only 50m uphill on the road find a path on the left which zigzags over Puy Mary's NE rib and meets

The airy ridge-top traverse to the Puy de Peyre Arse (L)

Here a 360° vista is gained of the major Cantal peaks.

the road again after 400m by dropping down to a small **parking area**. Cross the road and look out for a red way-marker, step over a fence to join an unlikely yet excellent path which leads up pleasantly to the rear of the bar at the **Pas de Peyrol**.

> The **Pas de Peyrol** has a tourist information office, a trinket shop, public toilets and a café.

Shorter Alternative Route

This route starts with the latter part of Walk 3 in reverse. From the Pas de Peyrol walk SW down the **D680** towards Col de Serre for about 100m. Here pick up a path on the right which traverses above the road for 200m before splitting. Take the right hand fork which leaves the road and swings around the hillside beneath the Puy Mary to meet the main ridge path down from Mary's summit at the mountain's SE shoulder and at the start of the **Brêche de Rolland** ridge. Continue following the main route as described until the point at which the return path leaves the ridge before the rocky summit slopes of Peyre Arse. Return from this point following the directions for the main route.

WALK 5
Around Medieval Murat

Start/Finish	Tourist office in main square of Murat
Distance	7km
Ascent	380m
Grade	1
Time	2hrs 30mins
Max Altitude	1192m
Map	IGN 1:25,000 Sheet 2435OT *Monts du Cantal*
Public Transport	Train to Murat
Parking	Plenty of free parking areas off the N112 in the town, and two lots of public toilets

This is a superb outing taking in the environs of Murat. It is a perfect antidote to a day spent hiking the higher Cantal summits, yet gives a surprising sense of being in the countryside despite never venturing too far from civilisation.

Highlights of the route include the plentiful birds-eye views of local churches and chateaux in addition to the unique 12th century chapel of St Anthony built on the eye-catching rocky hill of the same name. The route also incorporates a visit to the impressive hilltop Madonna that stands aloft a cliff of basalt columns and overlooks Murat.

Start from the tourist office in the main square, where there is also a car park. Follow the road to the post office and go right. After 50m some steps lead up to a pharmacy. Take these and turn left at the top, reaching Murat's medieval **church**.

> **Murat** itself is is a good base for exploring the Cantal, having all amenities and accommodation, as well as a train station.

At the church turn right following the little Madonna plaques up steps and then a small street. Statue signs and various other waymarkers guide you uphill. These can be followed rightwards to the road and straight across at a

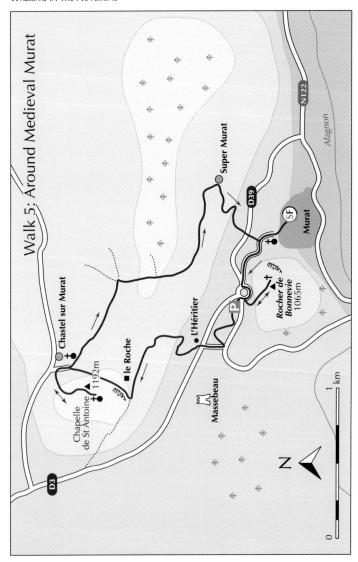

Walk 5: Around Medieval Murat

N122

Alagnon

Super Murat

D39

SF

Murat

Chastel sur Murat

L'Héritier

Rocher de
Bonnevie
1065m

P

le Roche

1192m

Chapelle
de St Antoine

Massebeau

D3

N

1 km

0

crossroads, passing an old lemonade bottling premises. On reaching a track find a signpost for the St James Way. Go along the track, gaining height and snaking around the hill. Take an obvious left up a wide path to the **Rocher de Bonnevie**, with its Madonna statue.

At the statue, actually called Notre Dame de la Haute Auvergne, a **cross** commemorates a pilgrimage to Jerusalem. Care should be taken if circumnavigating the statue as it perches very close to the cliff's edge.

From the statue, retrace your steps down the hill then head across the road to the parking area by the roundabout. ▶ Exit this at its far left side, following a small lane swinging round the bottom of some houses. This becomes a grassy track which offers brief views of the **Massebeau** château. At a junction with a gravel track turn left and after 50m reach the main road, which is crossed to climb some stone steps opposite and the track beyond. This is signposted with the yellow and blue St James Way markers once again. Go through a gate and after 100m turn right on another track. Continue along this as it passes a barn and through another gate. Here an overgrown path signed to 'Chastel sur Murat' branches off left: take this. ▶

Amble along the narrow path towards the crags of the Chapelle St Antoine hill passing another gate after 100m. To the right the church of Chastel sur Murat comes into view, soon to be joined by glimpses of the armadillo-armour basalt lava formations jutting out of the hillside. Pass the ruins of **le Roche** on your right. Here the path splits. Take the higher grassy path and reach a gate beneath the basalt columns. A short detour left will give better views of these.

Go through the gate and soon climb above le Roche. Upon reaching the village head towards the church, then take the road left looking out for a signed track to **Chapelle St Antoine**. Having passed through a short section of woods the path doubles back uphill and winds up to the chapel.

There are two benches and a useful water filling station here.

Look out for an ancient carved crucifix in a field to your left.

Notre Dame de la Haute Auvergne watches over Murat

The 12th century **chapel** is nestled on a small plateau, the Roc St Antoine, which provides a natural
fortress due to its basalt bastions. Archaeologists
have found evidence of settlements here dating
from the Neolithic period to the Middle Ages and
there have been particularly interesting finds from
the time of the Roman conquest discovered on the
rocky mount.

The chapel boasts a 14th century red and
yellow mural of the bishop and the Virgin Mary.
Martins can also be found nesting inside on col-
umn ledges. There are good views from the top
of the hill, where a number of Cantal peaks such
as the distinctive trapezoid of the Plomb can be
spied.

Leaving the chapel, retrace your steps to the church
at **Chastel sur Murat**. Here take the track on the right S
side of the church which provides pleasant level hiking.
Continue to where the track appears to come to an end
at orange markers and take a right on a path into a field.
This climbs up towards a pine forest which is passed on
its right. The path swings round the hillside descending
gradually above Super Murat and soon joins a track at a
farm building.

At a sign for the Sentier de Giou, ignore a left turn
and instead continue straight on leading into the houses
of **Super Murat**, following orange waymarkers on lamp-
posts with 'Retour' and dog pawprints on them. These
lead you right and down a track to join the **D39**. Follow
this right for 20m, then bear left on a path downhill back
to the centre of town.

WALK 6
The Plomb du Cantal

Start/Finish	Les Gardes near St Jacques des Blats
Distance	11km (13km from St Jacques)
Total Ascent	750m (950m from St Jacques)
Difficulty	3
Time	4hrs 30mins (5hrs 15mins from St Jacques)
Highest Point	1855m
Map	IGN 1:25,000 Sheet 2435OT *Monts du Cantal*
Public Transport	Bus to St Jacques
Parking	Parking area on the hairpin bend at the bottom of Les Gardes

As the highest summit in the Cantal, the Plomb demands attention. Despite the fact that the entire Monts du Cantal area forms part of the same ancient supervolcano, the Plomb is set apart from the other principal peaks of the range. The Plomb hosts the ski resort of Lioran on its slopes but the beauty of our route is that evidence of this remains largely hidden for most of the hike. The views from the upper reaches are particularly expansive and the route up the Arpon du Diable or Devil's Harpoon provides a dramatic approach to the main summit. This is a challenging walk demanding good navigation and fitness.

St Jacques des Blats has a campsite and a bar/restaurant. Along the D559 south of St Jacques there is a hotel. For those starting here the best option is to simply follow the marked minor road up to Les Gardes. A track appearing on the map to lead there via Ferval is not recommended because of cattle and excessive fences.

This is a key
landmark to avoid
ending up on the
wrong path.

From the parking area on the hairpin bend at the bottom of **Les Gardes** head uphill. After 60m pass a turnoff to Veyriére, where a sign for the Plomb is also marked. Ignore this and continue to another sign pointing left for the Arpon du Diable – unfortunately this good signage does not continue so care needs to be taken with route finding. About 60m later, at an old mill wheel, take the track branching off right downhill. ◄ The track swings

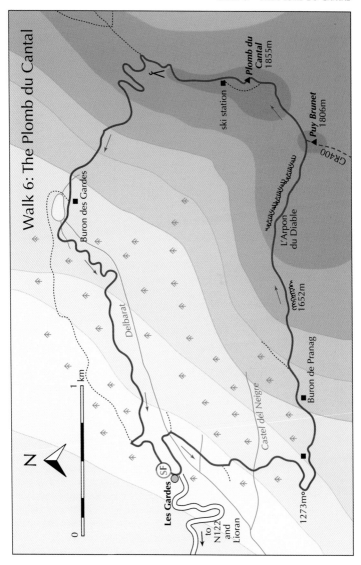

Walk 6: The Plomb du Cantal

The Plomb du Cantal from the summit of the Devil's Harpoon

down to a river where it momentarily doubles back on itself rightwards before crossing a bridge. Having crossed this, ignore a minor path leftwards and follow the main path rightwards parallel to the stream initially and then uphill. Green waymarkers can be found on this section of the route by the observant.

The path now winds its way up through woodland. After 1km the path splinters. Take the right fork leading to a boulder filled **stream** and follow more green markers. Soon a path branches right downhill. Take the left option steeply up through the forest and continue to keep eyes peeled for the reassuring green markers. The path gains the ridge crest of l'Arpon du Diable at **1273m**. After 100m on the ridge the woods peter out and you will be suddenly rewarded with expansive views.

Pass a ruin on its right side and then the **Buron de Pranag**. After a further 100m stay on a less distinct path which follows the ridge crest, ignoring a more pronounced path which descends left. Head directly towards the crags of the Arpon. A pesky barbed wire fence must be negotiated by dipping under the wire at a place where the land has been dug out for the benefit of hikers. Do

not be perturbed and rest assured that this is a permissive route. Roughly 80m above the fence a cairn is passed and the path becomes much easier to follow. The route passes to the left of the steepest rocks and cairns mark the way. ▶ Keep skirting to the left of the **rocks** (marked at **1652m** on the map) until a saddle on the ridge crest can be accessed.

Continue up the spine to the upper **rocks** of the Arpon. Having gained the **Arpon** the gradient becomes steadier. Another fence is crossed. The ridge becomes sharper and though lofty, is never overly exposed. Happy hiking leads to the Arpon's summit. Peak-baggers may now want to deviate to the nearby **Puy Brunet** but most will march directly towards the Plomb, joining the ancient Roman road of the **GR400** to do so. On reaching the foot of the Plomb's trapezoid summit, take a path which forks right and follow it round to the **summit**.

On a clear day the lucky hiker may be rewarded with distant glimpses of the **Alps** to the E and perhaps the **Pyrenees** to the S. The summit has two orientation tables to assist the eagle-eyed.

The Puy Griou from the Buron de Pranag

In summer many pansies bloom here.

63

From the summit follow the wooden steps down to the **ski station**. ◄ At the ski station, the Buron des Gardes route is clearly signed. Keeping to the brow of the hill for 200m and passing the start of a few ski runs you will pass a pylon covered in dishes, 50m beyond this branch left off the track, dipping under a wire fence and ensuring you follow a green sign to the Buron des Gardes. Initially the route cuts back towards the pylon, taking wide grassy switchbacks downhill marked with green paint. The pleasant switchbacks come to an abrupt end as you reach a streambed under the cable car wires, but the green markers continue intermittently to guide your way. Head towards the nearby lake winding down left over a watercourse.

The refuge here is closed during summer.

Just before reaching the lake, pass through another electric fence which has plastic shock-guards on it for access. Pass the man-made lake on the left side in order to explore the photogenic stone arch and an untidy **buron** once used as a refuge. The path peters out a little at this side but a better path is joined at the SW corner of the lake.

> **Burons** are the remnants of a pastoral way of life. In medieval times, they were just hollows made in the mountainside whose openings were covered with branches and thatch or clumps of turf in the walls. This system was gradually replaced by burons built of stone with slate roofs. The burons were only occupied for five months of the year when they gave shelter to cowherds grazing their cattle on the high slopes. The cowherds made the traditional cheeses Cantal and Salers on site.

Roughly 60m below the lake a track leaves left. Take this down the catchment of the **River Delbarat**. This soon leads to a gate with a green marker and descends steadily through the woods. On reaching a crossroads of tracks take the left way down to Les Gardes, ignoring a signpost pointing Les Gardes in the opposite direction. The track leads directly back to the village and our starting point.

WALK 7

A Rombière Ramble

Start/Finish	Parc de Volcans d'Auvergne parking between Pas de Peyrol and Mandailles
Distance	5km
Total Ascent	200m
Difficulty	1
Time	1hr 20mins
Highest Point	1370m
Map	IGN 1:25,000 Sheet 2435OT *Monts du Cantal*
Public Transport	Buses run to Mandailles 4km away

This short ramble explores the uppermost part of the beautiful glacial valley of the Jordanne River and delves into the heart of the Cirque de Mandailles. The Jordanne is one of twelve valleys radiating from the hub of the supervolcano of the Cantal. The route takes the hiker past several burons – mountain shelters formerly used by cowherds for cheesemaking.

The **parking area** has a picnic bench and an information board. From here take the track heading NE, parallel to the **Jordanne River** and passing a ski-cabin. ▶ After walking 800m through woodland there will be a **building** on your left. Here the track swings sharply back right, crossing the Jordanne. In 100m take a signposted track left marked in blue to the Sources of the Jordanne. Continue for 200m to cross some of the 'sources' or small tributaries of the Jordanne. After a steep rise pass through a gateway.

The Puy Griou and its smaller sister peak le Griounou loom spectacularly to the right.

The **beech forests** of the Cirque des Mandailles grow mainly on the vertiginous north faces of the mountains, whereas the southerly slopes of the hills are largely clear leaving ideal pasture. The beech served as fuel for heating dwellings in the Jordanne

65

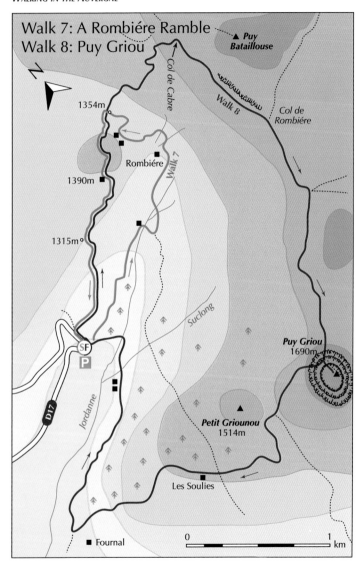

Walk 7: A Rombiére Ramble
Walk 8: Puy Griou

Puy Bataillouse

Col de Cabre

Walk 8

Col de Rombiére

1354m

Rombiére

Walk 7

1390m

1315m

Suclong

Puy Griou
1690m

SF
P

Jordanne

D17

Petit Griounou
1514m

Les Soulies

Fournal

0   1

km

*The head of the
Jordanne valley*

valley and was also used to make clogs and to build
railways.

Many of the old forestry tracks are open today
and are used for Nordic skiing in the winter. Beech
does not thrive above 1450m, where bilberry
bushes take its place.

Swinging rightwards out of the woods, the Puy de
Peyre Arse and its ridge down to the Col de Cabre come
into view. **Rombière** itself appears 100m later – a *buron*
building with a blue roof. Passing the ruined dwelling of
Rombière the path going left is initially difficult to follow. Head in the direction of another visible *buron* and
it soon becomes more obvious. Descend a little and go
through a squeeze gate to the *buron*. Shortly afterwards
a sign marks the Col de Cabre right, but a wide track left
is our way back.

The track back provides lovely fast hiking and gives
good views of your outbound hike. After 1.5km of easy
hiking, and just before reaching the road take a left down
a well-maintained path which niftily avoids the road and
leads directly to the parking area.

WALK 8
Puy Griou

Start/Finish	Parc de Volcans d'Auvergne parking between Pas de Peyrol and Mandailles
Distance	12.5km
Total Ascent	750m
Difficulty	3
Time	4hrs 30mins
Highest Point	1690m
Map	IGN 1:25,000 Sheet 2435OT *Monts du Cantal*
Public Transport	Buses run to Mandailles 4km away

It is not possible to visit the Cantal without being impressed by the sharp pyramidical form of the Puy Griou. As the steepest summit of the range, the dangerous-looking Griou attracts the eye but appears unnerving and prohibitive. In fact the Griou is overcome by an ascent which is no more difficult than that of the Lake District's Skiddaw.

That said, the Griou's summit does feel tremendously lofty, like an eagle's perch from which to survey the rest of the volcanic range. The approach is from the Jordanne valley – one of the most picturesque areas of the Cantal.

See map for Walk 7

Fast hiking with occasional breaks in the trees giving glimpses of the delights to come is the order here.

To start the route take the green waymarked path to the Col de Cabre, heading uphill into the woods from the parking area on a path between a signpost and the ski hut. After 100m reach a wider track and turn right up this. ◀ After 1.5km and with a little gradual descent pass a couple of *burons* to your right and, always aiming for the col at the head of the valley, pick up a good path with red waymarkers, which passes through a gate after 400m. In summer lovely buttercups, violets and broom flowers decorate your ascent to the **Col de Cabre**.

Head through a gate at the col then take a right on the most worn route towards the signposted Griou. The path now brilliantly contours round the S face and crags of the

The magnificent Griou from the Col de Cabre

Puy Bataillouse, after which it is joined by another trail from Téton de Vénus at the **Col de Rombiére**. Continue on the superb traversing path to approach the Puy Griou, where a signpost proclaims a 30 minute round trip to the summit.

The path ascends steeply up scree and rock. The way could be described as a very easy scramble similar to Yorkshire's Pen-y-ghent, but most people will not require the use of their hands. Follow cairns for the best route. The **summit of Puy Griou** boasts two larger cairns, disconcerting drops and exceptional views.

69

The Griou is composed of a cone of **phonolite volcanic rock**, which is supposed to ring when tapped
on its surface. The mountain formed the chimney
of the supervolcano from which the Cantal range
was formed.

Ignore arrows pointing an alternative way back, simply return the way you came to the signpost at the foot of
the Griou. ◄

On meeting the original path turn left on the GR
route to Mandailles and Gliziou. The path passes 300m
later between the Griou and its little sister the Grionou
by a ruin then crosses a V stile. Negotiating the W face
of Griou the path reaches a junction. Turn off the GR
route here to head straight down the hill on a less walked
path where there are some discontinuous green markers. Descend into trees to cross a stream then follow the
overgrown track straight ahead ignoring a path appearing
from the left. Eventually reach a clear track and PR signs.
Here turn right. The track is grassy but becomes rockier
then crosses an unpaved road and continues down. ◄

Do not attempt to cut
the corner here as
erosion is a problem.

By turning right on
the unpaved road
a slightly easier
but somewhat
monotonous return to
the parking area can
be made.

At **les Soulies** ruins (1225m) the track becomes a
path and offers views of the Puy Chavaroche. Soon after
this point an openable electric fence must be negotiated.
This may not be a permanent fixture but do not let it
phase you – it is completely normal and not there to stop
hikers. The path dips into the woods, swinging right with
some sparse waymarkers. Head to the bottom of an open
grassy area above the Soulies ruin. Stay at the right edge
of the pasture while descending. This section does have
difficult route-finding, a little patience and attention will
help. The path becomes vague as it heads down a tongue
of hillside just to the left of the trees but the rooftop of the
Fournal gîte soon comes into view.

As soon as this is spotted a partially hidden green
waymarker guides walkers to a path going right. Take this
path down into the la Blatte de Bos woods. If you find
yourself too close to the building at Fournal you have
missed the path, so go right from the pasture through
the trees to meet the path after 20–30m. Follow the path

through the woods to intersect a wide clear track and turn right downhill. Ignore two tracks coming from the left and follow the route marked with green signs to the Col de Cabre. This ascends slightly to the **buildings** marked at 1095m and a stream crossing. After 100m take the left fork down a steep descent to the **Suclong** river and a wooden bridge. Cross this and 100m further on cross the larger **Jordanne** river at a second bridge. Continue snaking up the wooded hillside steeply from the river. This brutal 150m of ascent is a real sting in the tail. It is signed with VTT markers and meets the track near the **parking area**.

WALK 9
Up the Usclade

Start/Finish	Col du Pertus parking area off D317 St Jacques to Mandailles
Distance	7km
Ascent	260m
Grade	2
Time	2hrs
Max Altitude	1498m
Map	IGN 1:25,000 Sheet 2435OT *Monts du Cantal*
Public Transport	Bus to Mandailles then 3km to the pass

The trip to the top of the Puy de l'Usclade is one of the few there and back routes included in this book. Although retracing your steps has its disadvantages, there is no obvious round trip to be made on this mountain and the Usclade excursion should not be missed. Routefinding is easy and this is a carefree ramble where the views are surprisingly good considering the amount of woodland on route. The wooded sections give the particular benefit of shade on a hot day. It is worth considering hiking the shorter route to the Elancèze summit on the same day, doubling up on routes from both the N and S sides of the Col du Pertus, with perhaps a cheese and wine picnic in between.

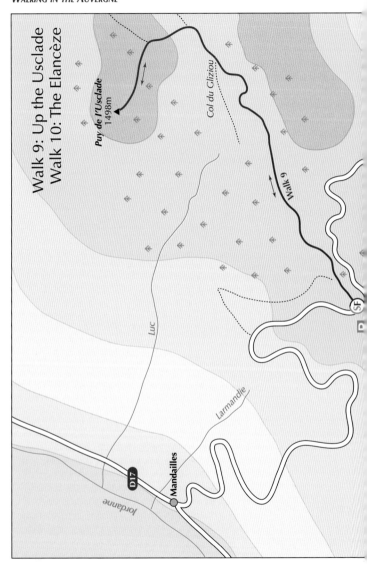

Walk 9: Up the Usclade
Walk 10: The Elancèze

Puy de l'Usclade
1498m

Col du Gliziou

Walk 9

Luc

Larmandie

Jordanne

Mandailles

D17

SF

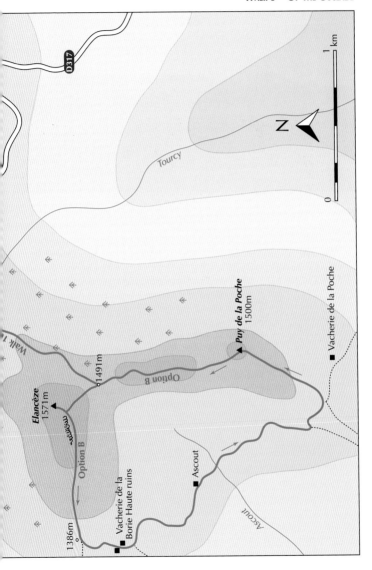

Looking north towards Walk 4 and the Brêche de Rolland area from Usclade's summit

From the **Col de Pertus parking area** take the obvious path N. After 200m turn right on a path branching off the main track, signposted Puy Griou and with red and white waymarkers. ◄ The path soon starts to climb and care should be taken not to branch off: most potential mistakes are marked with red crosses on trees. The path eventually swings around the head of the Luc river and presents the SW rampart of Puy de l'Usclade. Crossing the large basin of Luc tributaries, the path loses a substantial amount of height on some open pasture before a gate allows you to re-enter the wood with a large track visible below.

This path flickers through woodland giving occasional views of the conical Griou.

Views of the Puy Chavaroche at the opposite side of the Jordanne valley accompany the hiker as the path continues to swing around the basin towards the Col du Gliziou. After 300m join a more prominent route and continue straight ahead, climbing to the **Col du Gliziou** at 1350m. At the col follow a signposted route left to Puy Griou and Usclade.

At a hairpin bend 250m later, branch off left on a clear path, ignoring various coloured crosses at this point. This is the spur leading to the summit of the Usclade through beech woods. The path briefly becomes bouldery but cairns guide the way to the **summit**. ◄

The small flat area on the Usclade summit gives stunning 360° panoramic views of all the major Cantal peaks.

From the summit, return the way you came up. Red markers should aid hikers on the return to the **Col du Pertus**.

WALK 10
The Elancèze

Start/Finish	Col du Pertus parking area off D317 St Jacques to Mandailles
Distance	3km return (longer circuit 8km)
Total Ascent	270m (longer circuit 500m)
Difficulty	1 (longer circuit grade 3)
Time	1hr 15mins (longer circuit 3hrs)
Highest Point	1571m
Map	IGN 1:25,000 Sheet 2435OT *Monts du Cantal*
Public Transport	Bus to Mandailles then 3km to the pass

The Elancèze is a popular and straightforward destination from the Col du Pertus. Its two craggy summits give splendid views of the principal peaks of the Cantal and down to Mandailles in the Jordanne valley. Walkers wishing for a simple hike should therefore visit the summits and return via the outbound route. Those looking for a bit more adventure should take the worthwhile but tricky longer circuit. This second option is definitely reserved for experienced hillwalkers only – two sections are on permitted routes without proper paths and navigation can prove difficult. The preponderance of inquisitive dairy cattle in the Ascout area of the route may also make some walkers think twice. The longer circuit does reward the effort with more ridge walking, seclusion and views of the Elancèze from both the N and S sides however.

From the **parking area** head S on an obvious path, passing through a gate and going uphill, initially through meadows and then woodland. It has red and white waymarkers. The col at **1491m** is reached with little fuss. ▶

From the col turn right following a fence up towards the **rocky summit of the Elancèze**. The path takes a rib up the summit ridge and swings right to reach the actual summit, which has no markers but does boast an excellent vantage point.

A small detour can be made to the **second rocky summit** of the Elancèze.

See map for Walk 9

Sensational views of the Griou, Peyre Arse and Plomb give resting hikers a treat here.

A new use for an old van at Ascout

From the second summit, walkers can retrace their steps all the way back to the Col du Pertus.

Extension: Round trip via Puy de la Poche (Option B)

From the second summit of the Elancèze follow the clear ridge path heading W and with the **Vacherie de la Borie Haute ruins** visible beneath you. Take note of these as you will soon pass amongst them.

The ridge crest path descends into woods, with green waymarkers temporarily guiding walkers through the trees to eventually reach a more defined arête. At the **1386m** saddle the main path goes straight on towards the Roc du Chauve through a gate. Our route takes a left down and out of the woods to the pasture, without a proper path. Head towards the **ruins**, which should be visible from here, on the left hand side of a stream. Go between the two sets of ruins to join a track and turn left. Frustratingly the track soon comes to an abrupt end. Continue descending in order to cross the stream in front of you near a lone beech tree. Here a very faint right-trending path can be followed uphill past another solitary beech to the top right hand corner of the pasture where the woods are re-entered. There is an orange waymarker on a rock 30m before entering the woods. Here the path surprisingly becomes distinct, with more markers. Descend for 50m in order to enter a small clearing. Here turn left through a break in a fence and follow a track which leads round the hillside. Occasional old waymarkers are reassuring.

A fence now appears to bar the way but is easily negotiated beside a beech tree with an orange marker. ▶ Next pass a small buttress of rock, which has an identifiable human face, and continue to the ruined **Ascout** *buron*, where an old ruined van has become a wood store.

Leaving the woods the buron at Vacherie de la Poche is visible far ahead.

The Elancèze summit from the longer variant

Salers cows roam these hills and are the reason behind the unlikely fences on some of the Cantal routes. The cows can sometimes be 'overfriendly'. Do not be alarmed if large groups approach you. Some firm movements and deep-voiced shouts usually disperse them, waving a staff or stick seems effective.

From here the track is difficult to find but clear once joined. This descends gradually and after 200m the **river Ascout** can be crossed beside some large concrete tubes. Cross the river and negotiate another fence, either by opening it or ducking under. The track now improves and climbs through the woods towards another visible *buron*. Look out for a path branching left when the track levels out. Take this to exit the woods. Do not go to the *buron* or the higher **Vacherie de la Poche**. Instead continue to the crest of the hill where a fence is crossed, the GR400 is joined and views are gained of the Elancèze ridge. Where the path meets the GR route there is a signpost. Here go leftwards steadily uphill on the right of the fence towards **Puy de la Poche**.

Way-finding is now easy and the summit is gained after 700m or so. Should you find yourself on the track to the left of the fence, worry not, merely look out for a break in the fence near the Poche summit and cross back to the GR route.

From Puy de la Poche the route is straightforward and follows the ridge N on a clear path with several rocky outcrops until joining your outbound route at the **1491m** col.

WALK 11

Puy Violent and the Shadow Rock

Start/Finish	Récusset on the D37 off the N side of the D680 Pas de Peyrol road
Distance	14km
Total Ascent	760m
Difficulty	3
Time	5hrs
Highest Point	1633m
Map	IGN 1:25,000 Sheet 2435OT *Monts du Cantal*
Public Transport	There is a limited bus service to Récusset from Salers
Parking	4 spaces off the D37 at a hairpin bend in Récusset, more along route
Accommodation	The village of Récusset has two large auberges and gîte accommodation

Puy Violent is the westernmost of the major Cantal peaks and has a suitably remote feel. The easiest ascent involves a tedious and difficult drive around to a high parking area at the W side of the mountain from where a track ascends the least dramatic flank of Violent. Far more rewarding is a much longer circuit of the mountain and its higher sister the Roc des Ombres from the small village of Récusset. By taking this option, the hiker will understand how the mountain has earned its menacing name. While Puy Violent is not the highest point of the day, it is the most significant and distinctive peak on the route. The ridge blooms with gentians in summer.

There are four parking spaces off the **D37** at a hairpin bend in the village of **Récusset**, and a large wooden figure of a hiker. From the **parking area** walk along the road uphill for 30m then take a surfaced road right, signposted to Puy Violent.

There is more parking available 100m along this minor road. Pass an auberge and shortly afterwards turn right on a path crossing a stile. This descends to the **Maronne river**, which is crossed by way of a wooden

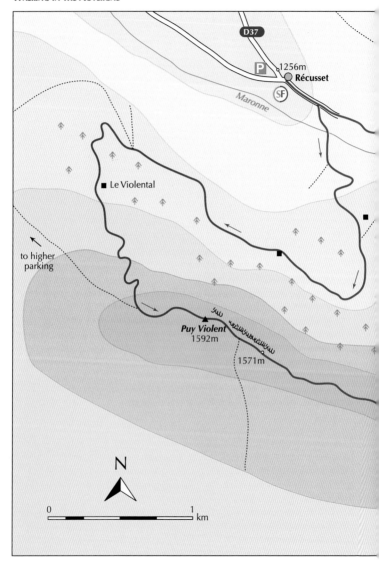

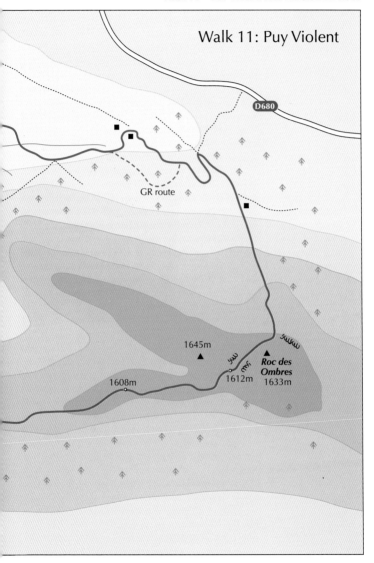

Walk 11: Puy Violent

D680

GR route

1645m
▲

Roc des Ombres
1633m

1612m

1608m

*Informative little men
in the Gué valley*

This section of the route is part of a heritage trail and has several signs explaining the history of farming in the region.

bridge. At a third stile the path splits. Here follow yellow waymarkers leftwards on a path which can often be muddy. Cross two converging streams and continue leftwards uphill, passing three horse troughs. After 300m the faint path swings back on itself across the hillside, giving views of the Col de Néronne and Récusset. ◄

After ascending towards woods a *buron* is passed on your left, where there is a picnic bench. Cross a stile and turn right along a wide track to skirt the source of the River Bouge. After 1.2km the track emerges from the woods passing a **farmhouse** to the left and gaining views of the Roc de Labro near the Col de Néronne across the valley.

A path that appears on the IGN map to climb from here more directly to the Puy Violent summit does not exist on the ground. Our track becomes rougher and after a further 2km, including a small amount of descent, this forks and the left branch is taken uphill to Puy Violent and buron **le Violental**. Climb on this track through the woods. Cross over a stile and 100m later pass the Violental buron on its right. ▶

Above this buron there is another ruin. The track bends round towards this but take a path which heads straight up, cutting off the dogleg and rejoining the track for 40m until an indistinct path with red and white markers comes off to the left, just after crossing a stream. The path is grassy over open terrain. Follow the waymarkers until a stile crosses an electric fence, where our path is joined by the large track from the high W side parking area. Any fresh-faced hikers met here are undoubtedly coming from there.

Approaching the conical summit of Puy Violent the track splits. Take the grassy path branching left over a stile and heading directly to the summit which is marked by a granite IGN block and a series of cairns.

> The **summit of Puy Violent** is a grand place from which to lap up the views, giving one off perspectives of the Puy Mary and your higher objective the Roc des Ombres or Shadow Rock, along with Puy Chavaroche, Puy de Peyre Arse and the Plomb du Cantal in the far distance.

Follow the path over the crest of Puy Violent down to a single wire fence, which is easily negotiated. Keep to the right of the fence down into the col between Violent and the unnamed peak at 1571m. Stay on the crest and follow the path climbing to the lofty **1571m** vantage point. Remain on the right of a fence descending from this summit and pass through another wire fence with a hook-handle before continuing uphill on a wide grassy path

As the path climbs up to the Roc des Ombres, the high mountain with a rocky summit to the right is Puy Chavaroche. Excellent hiking on a beautiful ridge leads up to the **1608m spot height**, then dips away to the right traversing the hillside below the highest point of the ridge at **1645m**, bypassing its awkward rocky summit. As the

This buron would make a suitable bivvy spot, although high cattle grazing means that stream water from the area should not be drunk.

path forks left away from the wire fence, the Enfloquet ruins are visible beneath you to the right.

Near the 1612m spot height cross a small stream and traverse the steep but not overly exposed hillside. The path dips and then climbs through a photogenic rocky gateway which delivers you to the left side of the ridge. The route now traverses the N side of the **Roc des Ombres** to join another path heading steeply downhill. Do not cross the ridge crest again but go left down the path alongside a fence. The path is small but easy to follow down the upper part of the Maronne valley. A farm track joins our route from the right and reaches a distinctive **ruined buron** across the valley.

Here continue descending to a tiny col and then leave the path by dropping down left for roughly 60m until a level section of indistinct path is found. Head right here into the woods, following dispersed red way-markers. At the edge of the woods turn left, following waymarkers down to a boggy streambed. Cross two streams to find a clearer route with markers turning right and heading down the main valley. The path crosses more streams and does not enter the woods but goes through a metal gate.

Head straight on here along a clear track which leaves the path to the right marked with a red cross. The GR400 continues along the leftwards path but this becomes unpleasantly waterlogged as it crosses numerous tributaries, and the right hand option along the track is recommended for those wanting to keep their thighs dry. Follow the level track for 400m to a **ruined buron**: just beyond this at another ruin leave the path and head left downhill beside a wall, crossing a small streambed to meet a rubbly track after 200m or so. Take this right, rejoining the GR waymarkers and thus avoiding the worst of the wet feet territory.

After 150m on this track do not cross a wooden stile but continue down the valley. Go through a gate next to a second decrepit stile. Turn left here back towards the river and a wooden bridge. The rough track eventually meets the road and deposits you in **Récusset**.

WALK 12
Roche Taillade and Roc d'Hoziéres

Start/Finish	Parking area on D17 2km SW of Pas de Peyrol
Distance	6km
Ascent	290m
Grade	1 or 2 (depending on summits visited)
Time	1hr 45mins (2hrs 15mins with deviation to summit of Taillade)
Max Altitude	1654m or 1614m
Map	IGN 1:25,000 Sheet 2435OT *Monts du Cantal*
Public Transport	Train to Murat and taxi

This hike takes in some magnificent volcanic rock scenery and ridge walking without a huge struggle to gain height. The steep yet rounded dome of Roc d'Hoziéres is reminiscent of California's Yosemite and the ridge crest feels much wilder and more isolated than that of the neighbouring Puy Mary.

The route starts from a hairpin bend with parking for six cars high up on the Pas de Peyrol road. If this layby is full the nearest available parking would be at the pass and this would unfortunately entail a 1.5km trudge on tarmac to reach the path. The ascent of the Roc d'Hoziéres benefits from a late start as the afternoon sun highlights the pyramid form of Puy Mary beautifully.

Leave the **parking** layby, taking the route around the north of **la Chapeloune** (1686m). At the start of the path there is a fork signing the Chavaroche left, but take the right hand route. The path climbs gradually, passing a grassy nose at a solitary wooden stake with a yellow way-marker on it. ▶

Peace and tranquillity are found here, enabling full appreciation of the sublime buttresses of volcanic rock. After a kilometre join the GR route on the ridge crest, with surprisingly little effort. A path taking the right hand route around the **Roche Taillade** is obvious and splits off after a further 1km. Take this wide path, without much exposure, to pass beneath the mesa-like Taillade and

The Roche Taillade's craggy table-top and the Roc d'Hoziéres' scarily smooth face are drawn together to compose an enchanting view.

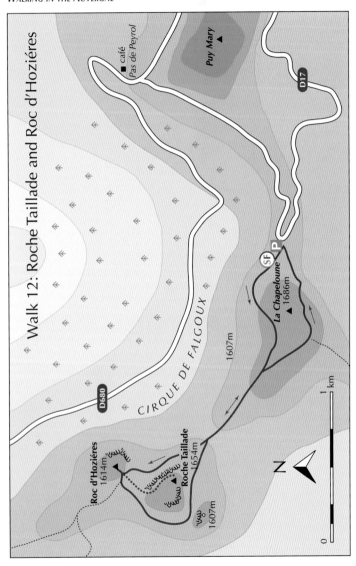

Walk 12: Roche Taillade and Roc d'Hoziéres

café
Pas de Peyrol

Puy Mary

D17

café
Pas de Peyrol

SF P

La Chapeloune
1686m

CIRQUE DE FALGOUX

D680

1607m

Roc d'Hoziéres
1614m

Roche Taillade
1654m

1607m

N

0   1 km

reach the col between Taillade and Roc d'Hoziéres. From this col both summits can be gained.

The **Roc d'Hoziéres** is a satisfying summit, gained in five minutes from the col. This gives a better view and is an easier ascent than that of Taillade. It is therefore strongly recommended. ▶ The Taillade path, conversely, is more exposed and requires care, especially in descent. If heading up Roche Taillade, avoid the left of the two paths, as it goes unnervingly close to the edge of Taillade's sheer crags. Unless you enjoy tightrope walking, we found it preferable for the most part to beat a track through the heather just to the right of this precarious path. ▶

A path goes down from the col in the direction of the Roc d'Ombres and the Enfloquet ruins to the NW. This trends round the back of the Roc de Hoziéres. At a red and white cross join the GR route beside a fence. Turn left and follow its red waymarkers gradually upwards to the wide col between Taillade and the rocks to the SW at **1607m**. ▶ Having swung round Taillade the GR route joins our ridge ascent route. Follow the GR path uphill to the Col de Redondet on the right S side of **la Chapeloune**. Stay on the main path and take it leftwards where it is

Approaching Roche Taillade and Roc d'Hoziéres

Include an extra 20 minutes for a trip to its summit, as time will be spent savouring the panorama from the top.

Allow an extra 20–30 minutes for a deviation to the summit of Taillade.

Here, 50m above the path, stands a lonely gendarme.

87

joined by the Puy Chavaroche path coming in from the right and beat a gradual descent to our starting point.

> The **Pas de Peyrol** is very popular with sadistic lycra-clad cyclists. It proves a great spot to marvel not only at the resilient iron-lunged kings and queens of the mountains, but also the forlorn and dejected bike-pushers who have bitten off more than they can chew.

WALK 13
Circuit of Puy Chavaroche

Start/Finish	Mandailles
Distance	13km
Total Ascent	900m
Difficulty	3
Time	4hrs 30mins–5hrs
Highest Point	1739m
Map	IGN 1:25,000 Sheet 2435OT *Monts du Cantal*
Public Transport	Bus to Mandailles
Parking	Parking area opposite Mandailles town hall

A grand and fulfilling hike through exquisite mountain scenery uncannily reminiscent of Snowdonia or the Lake District. The majestic and pleasantly gradual ridge crest provides a long and lofty approach to the Chavaroche summit and offers some of the finest hiking to be found in the Auvergne, amply rewarding those who have burnt off their cheese and pâté calories by venturing up steeply from Mandailles to reach it.

Mandailles has picnic benches by the river, public toilets, an auberge and a telephone. The described route could be reversed for those who prefer a more circuitous ascent, but there is method in the direction we describe which will preserve hikers' knees at the very least.

Start in **Mandailles**, at the parking area opposite the town hall on the SE side of the bridge.

Cross the bridge and turn left at the bus stop (public toilets here) and then immediately turn right, following the red waymarker. The route is signposted at a stone-carved crucifix dating back to 1658. Follow the road steeply to **Lasteyrie** (989m), through the upper part of the hamlet of Barugué. As you pass the last buildings there is a horse trough and a path directly uphill to Puy Chavaroche.

After 20m the path follows a slippery streambed for 30m. Take a left at a decrepit barn and contour around the hillside, then climb to the **1173m spot height**, following occasional green waymarkers. Go through a gate and straight uphill. Puy Chavaroche is now marked right – this will be our descent route so ignore it and continue straight uphill. Cross a faint farm track and head straight up the ridge, eventually entering some woods. ▸

The path swings right along the top of the woods. After 200m the fore-summits of Le Piquet (1580m) come into view. There is a huge gully N of the **1476m spot height**. Here the path splits. Take the left hand fork and follow green posts to gain the col beside le Piquet via numerous, relatively exposed, zigzags. Here the **GR400**

This is a steep and unrelenting ascent, but doing the circuit this way round prevents knee agony later and makes for a far more enjoyable gradual descent – try to bear this in mind as you huff and puff!

The northwest face of Puy Chavaroche

89

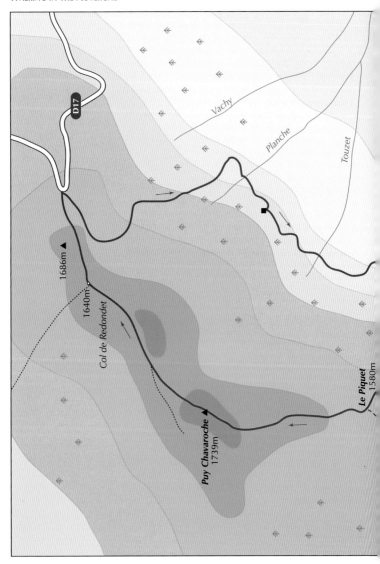

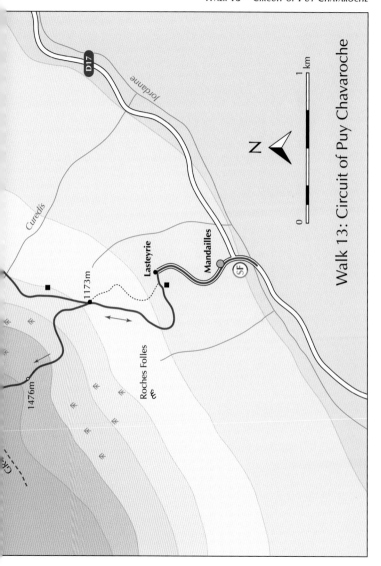

Walk 13: Circuit of Puy Chavaroche

joins and the path now goes over heathery ground following a fence. Follow red waymarkers up onto the ridge and do not branch off left. Fantastic hiking over the next kilometre leads to the **Puy Chavaroche** summit, where a wind shelter and large cairn await.

On leaving the peak, follow a clear path with red markers. After 100m switchback left to avoid a difficult step. The GR path now goes on the W side of the ridge but stay on the crest path for better views until reaching **Col de Redondet**. Here turn right and follow more red markers down to the **D17** road at a hairpin bend. Just before reaching the road take a right, doubling back on yourself beneath the way you came – this is signposted to Mandailles. At a fork after 20m take the descending route following green markers. The path eventually stops traversing and follows a rib into some trees crossing a stream after 200m. The route then works through lovely open pasture close to **la Planche river**. Cross this in woods and 50m later pass a **barn** on your left. Bob over the **Touzet river** then 500m further along pass some **burons** and shortly afterwards cross the **Curedis river**. Here the path splits. Take the right fork uphill signed to Mandailles. After 30m you will be joined by another track which is followed to the left. Look out for waymarkers in the trees. After 300m pass a **ruined barn** on your left and continue until reaching the place where the circuit began. Reverse your outbound route to Mandailles.

WALK 14

St Cirgues de Jordanne – Southern circuit

Start/Finish	Church in St Cirgues de Jordanne
Distance	6.5km
Total Ascent	270m
Difficulty	1
Time	2hrs 15mins
Highest Point	974m
Map	IGN 1:25,000 Sheet 2435OT *Monts du Cantal*
Public Transport	A bus runs along the D17 from Mandailles
Parking	Parking area off D17 on the N side of road by telephone box: also behind church to the left on entering the village from Pas de Peyrol

This pleasant amble is eminently suitable for those wanting a relaxed day after perhaps ticking off one of the more challenging high mountain routes in the area. The excursion winds its way around the mini-valleys of two Jordanne tributaries. It benefits from open pasture terrain, allowing marvellous views of the Puy Mary, Brêche de Rolland and Puy de Peyre Arse. The route could also easily be combined with Walk 15 (see extension below) to give a much longer outing, still starting from the pretty floral village of St Cirgues.

Start from the white cross at the **church**, where there is a blue sign. Follow this from the church, heading past an old bread oven on the right.

> **St Cirgues de Jordanne** is a pretty village where houses tend to be adorned with flowers. It has a hotel, a bar and a small shop. The village church dates from 1667 but looks even older than this.

The road soon becomes a track. Go right at a T junction after 100m. Pass beneath a hillside crucifix, continuing along the track and swinging right to cross a bridge

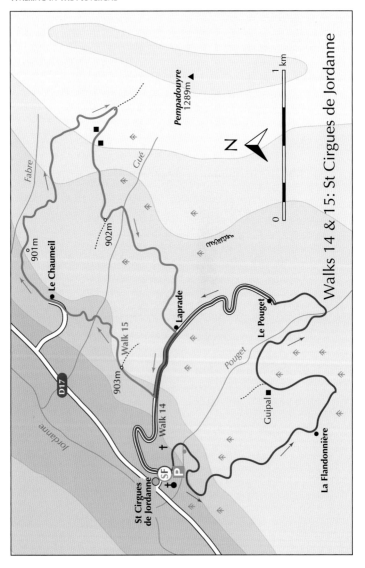

Walks 14 & 15: St Cirgues de Jordanne

St Cirgues de
Jordanne in bloom

over the small **Pouget river** in 300m, where small cascades froth among deciduous woodland. ▶ The route now leaves the track on a signposted path right to la Flandonnière.

From the bridge the craggy hills of Pempadouyre are seen to the left.

Continue uphill until a path with blue markers comes off to the left at a bend. Take this, gaining height through mixed woods, eventually joining a wide grassy path. Follow this left to the hamlet of **la Flandonnière**. Continue to follow blue markers through la Flandonnière. Pass through a gate beside the final dwelling, to find that the route now heads pleasantly downhill towards Guipal, looping around the hillside. There might well be an electric fence with a plastic hook-handle gate to negotiate on route to **Guipal**. At the farm follow blue markers and

Looking across the Pouget valley

ignore a track heading off downhill to your left. The main track swings rightwards briefly, crossing some open pasture before submerging you in dense woodland for 300m.

Eventually the **Pouget river** is crossed by way of a good wooden bridge. Beyond this, a yellow flap trail-bike gate awaits, as does the course of a stream, which the adept will negotiate without wetting toes. A choice of three paths, all of which lead to the same place, present themselves at the other side of the stream to switch hikers back uphill towards le Pouget hamlet: take the third path. After 100m a barn is passed to your left. The well used track continues to **le Pouget**, where a tarmac road offers uncomplicated trudging back down the hill to St Cirgues, passing through the pleasant hamlet of **Laprade** on route.

Do not be tempted to do Walk 15 in reverse as way-finding becomes especially complex in that direction.

Extension to Walk 15

For those wanting to link routes 14 and 15, go down the road for approximately 300m after Laprade and look out for a path with yellow markers turning right and follow the description for Walk 15 from this point. ◄

WALK 15
St Cirgues de Jordanne – Northern circuit

Start/Finish	Church in St Cirgues de Jordanne
Distance	6.5km
Total Ascent	380m
Difficulty	1
Time	2hrs 15mins
Highest Point	990m
Map	IGN 1:25,000 Sheet 2435OT *Monts du Cantal*
Public Transport	A bus runs along the D17 from Mandailles
Parking	Parking area off D17 on the N side of road by telephone box: also behind church to the left on entering the village from Pas de Peyrol

Although this walk starts with an unpromising spell on tarmac, it is a worthwhile outing in its own right as well as being an enjoyable extension to the previous adjacent route. If using this route to extend the circuit of Walk 14, do not be tempted to walk this route in reverse as way-finding becomes problematic in that direction. For those hiking clockwise as described, there are no such difficulties and the route is a good way to get better acquainted with the charms of the steep-sided Mandailles valley without exerting a mammoth amount of effort.

From the **church** head up the road through the village, ignoring a turnoff to the right. The minor road heads quite steeply around two big hairpin bends.

See map for Walk 14

> Coming up the road from the village there are a few **possible parking places** for those using a bit of initiative to cut out a little of the 1km of tarmac (if tempted to park along here, ensure adequate passing room for large farm vehicles).

Those on foot should look out for a large buttress of rock at the edge of the road about 1km beyond the village. Here find a yellow route-marker and go left up a track, which soon becomes a wide path. The path contours the

The tunnel of trees

Here small trees border each side of the path and give the effect of walking through a tunnel.

hillside through mixed woodland and makes a long gradual descent towards the **903m spot height**. At a fork in the path take the left way downhill, where the path narrows. Cross the **Gué river** (actually more of a stream) and ascend to the hamlet of **le Chaumeil**, where the path joins a surfaced road. Follow this downhill for 30m, then ignore a turning left and continue uphill to pass six water troughs on your right and head into the hamlet. The surfaced road becomes a track and passes pretty thatched buildings and a cross, before swinging left (NE) out of the hamlet.

The track continues gradually around the hillside and up the mini-valley of the **Fabre river**, where the scenery becomes wilder. After 1km upstream an obvious right turn with a yellow marker and a sign to Laprade is taken. Pass a **farm** to your left and follow a red sign to Laprade. From the farm the path trends down beside a fence, passing a **buron**. ◀ The path joins a track. Be careful not to miss a turnoff at the **902m spot height**. This turnoff to Laprade is made after 100m on the track and descends leftwards to the **Gué river**. There is a small easily missed sign to Laprade here.

After two wooden stiles and 200m the path leaves the watercourse and drier hiking through the woods is then enjoyed. Eventually the path becomes a wide farm track and winds around the hillside. After 300m on this level track take a left turn up a rubbly walled path, where there is a yellow waymarker. At the top of this chute a cattle feeder is passed. Head straight on along a path in a furrow beside an open field, then go through a marked gate to Laprade. Turn right on the main road at Laprade and return on it to **St Cirgues de Jordanne**.

THE CHÂINE DES PUYS
(MONTS DÔMES)

The lookout: The Chain of Puys from Puy de la Vache (Walk 17)

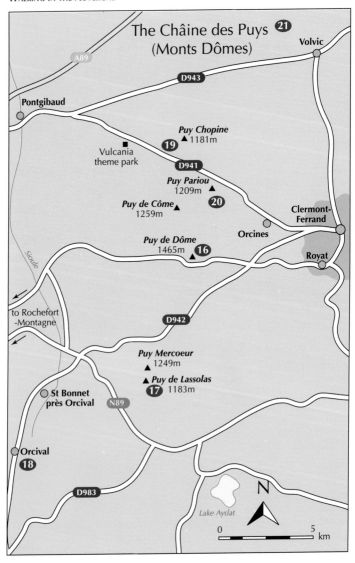

The Chaîne des Puys
(Monts Dômes) **21**

Volvic

A89

D943

Pontgibaud

Puy Chopine
19 ▲ 1181m

Vulcania
theme park

D941

Puy Pariou
1209m ▲

Puy de Côme ▲
1259m

20

Clermont-
Ferrand

Orcines

Puy de Dôme
1465m **16**
▲

Royat

to Rochefort
-Montagne

D942

Puy Mercoeur
▲ 1249m

▲ *Puy de Lassolas*
17 1183m

St Bonnet
près Orcival

N89

Orcival
18

D983

Lake Aydat

N

0   5
km

INTRODUCTION

'Steam puddings', 'bowler hats', 'nature's giant pimples' – call them what you will, the distinctively shaped volcanic summits of the Châine des Puys (also known as the Monts Dômes) provide a novel hiking area and are a must see sight, not only of the Auvergne, but of Western Europe. We have nothing like them in Britain, indeed, the verdant Puys here prove some of the finest examples of cinder or scoria cone volcanoes anywhere in the world, rivalling those of Central America. The Monts Dômes, like their near neighbours the Monts Dore, belong to the Parc Naturel Régional des Volcans d'Auvergne, which also includes the Artense and Cézallier plateaux and the Monts du Cantal. The famously bizarre and appealing Puy de Dôme which towers above Clermont-Ferrand is justifiably classified as a Grand Site of France. This gives a good vantage point from which to grasp the geography of the surrounding puys and their dimply craters. The town of Volvic gives a clue to the water quality and pristine nature of the landscape hereabouts. The numerous Puys of the Monts Dômes tend to stand in couples or isolation and lend themselves to short or medium length family-friendly walks.

The Monts Dômes cover a relatively small area, with the 40 links in the Châine des Puys lining up to the west of Clermont-Ferrand in a north–south procession about 4km wide and 45km long. The Puys are bordered to the south by the geologically distinct Monts Dore, and the modest distances between the two mini-ranges mean that it is most sensible to station one-self at a base convenient to both areas. A delightful choice is the lovely town of Orcival which nestles between the volcanic hills about 20km southwest of Clermont-Ferrand and roughly the same distance north of the spa town of Mont-Dore. Orcival's ornate basilica ensures that the town receives its fair share of visitors but it is not crowded and there are plentiful restaurants and shops selling local produce. The accommodation is varied, with both hotels and gîtes in town. For those camping, the nearby campsite at the tranquil village of St Bonnet (auberge, bakery, convenience store) provides wonderful views and is therefore recommended. Orcival was not on the public transport network at the time of writing and more sensible options for those without a car would be the towns of Volvic, Rochefort-Montagne and the major city of Clermont-Ferrand. The mountain town of Mont Dore could also be considered as a base for both the Châine des Puys and Monts Dore.

WALK 16
Puy de Dôme

Start/Finish	Col de Ceyssat
Distance	7.5km
Total Ascent	410m
Difficulty	2 (although steep, benches abound!)
Time	2hrs 15mins
Highest Point	1465m
Map	IGN 1:25,000 Sheet 2531ET *Chaîne des Puys*
Public Transport	In summer hourly buses run up to the col from Clermont-Ferrand
Parking	Parking area at Col de Ceyssat

Puy de Dôme is arguably the most famous site in the Auvergne and inspired the naming of one of the region's four *départements* in 1791. It towers impressively over the hub of Clermont-Ferrand and is consistently visible whenever any significant vantage point is gained across the massive region of the Auvergne.

Despite this fame, and being one of the 37 esteemed Grand Sites of France, the Puy de Dôme would certainly not win any prizes for being the most beautiful of the Auvergne's summits, adorned as it is with a huge communications mast poking out from its peak. However, the mountain's distinctive bowler hat shape, and steep, 20 per cent gradient slopes on every side make it an irresistible objective to hikers and tourists alike. Good paths and the expansive remains of a Roman temple on the top improve its allure. Until 2010 a toll road twisted around the Puy de Dôme, depositing motorists right on the top. Now this has been replaced by a costly tourist train, which will instead take those unwilling to put in the legwork up the hill to disembark at an underground station. More information is available at www.panoramiquedesdomes.fr.

The **Chemin des Muletiers** or Mule Drivers' Path is clearly signed from the car park, where there are two *auberges* and public toilets. A gravel path heads up steadily at first, then more steeply, zigzagging up the mountain. There are plenty of benches from which one can savour the

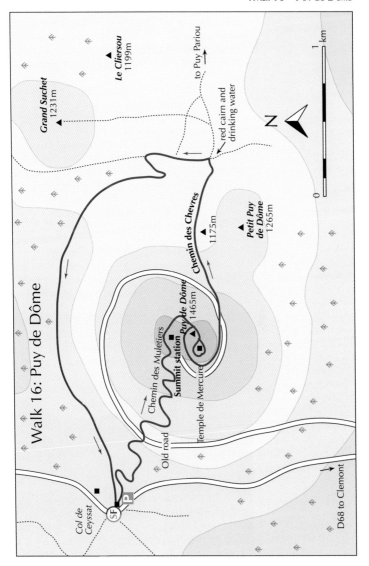

Walk 16: Puy de Dôme

Col de Ceyssat

Grand Suchet
1231m

Le Cliersou
1199m

to Puy Pariou

red cairn and
drinking water

Petit Puy
de Dôme
1265m

1175m

Chemin des Chevres

Summit station

Puy de Dôme
1465m

Chemin des Muletiers

Old road

Temple de Mercure

D68 to Clemont

N

1 km

0

plentiful views of the Châine des Puys and Monts Dore. The path negotiates a small line of cliffs and crosses the railway line once. It is surprisingly pleasurable hiking for such a contrived way.

> The **Puy de Dôme** is an extinct Pelean volcano, formed by two successive explosions of viscous lava which created the double dome about 10,800 years ago. Because the Puy de Dôme is first in line for receipt of cold air from the Atlantic, it has a similar climate to mountains more than 2000m higher and its summit is frozen for a third of the year.
>
> It may be diminutive, but the Puy de Dôme has always had pretensions of grandeur. The Auvergnat author Vialatte once boasted that the Dôme had a 'moral altitude' of 3500m. He added that locals should have no qualms about adding a measly 2000m to its height in order to impress the Swiss!

Near the **summit train station** the path becomes surfaced with concrete and curves left, joining a network of

The Puy de Dôme from Puy des Gouttes (Walk 19)

104

meandering paths round the large hilltop. To say that the views from the summit of Puy de Dôme are worth the effort would be superfluous when the French signage on the mountain puts it so theatrically: 'This boundless horizon inspires fear, your trembling eyes are afraid they will be lost in such an immeasurable expanse.'

In 1911 an intrepid pilot called **Eugene Renaux** made history by landing his plane named 'Farman' on the summit of Puy de Dôme. In doing so he secured a 100,000 Franc prize from the Michelin brothers, who wanted to further the development of aviation in their country. Renaux flew from Paris to the Dôme in less than six hours, to the amazement of the French populace.

Facilities at the **summit** include toilets, an emergency telephone, an observatory, a year-round picnic room and a seasonal café. There is little point being precious about the over-development here – it's nothing the British haven't seen before on Snowdon.

The **temple of Mercury** on the summit of Puy de Dôme dates back to the 1st or 2nd century, when the original buildings would have been visible from the Gallo-Roman capital of Augustonemetum (Clermont). The 2nd century is believed to have seen the start of a popular pilgrimage to the temple of Mercury from Lyon along Agrippa's Way. Mercury was the God of travellers. In the 19th century artefacts including a bronze statue of Mercury were found at the site, and as a result thorough excavations began.

The GR4 descent route starts from the road circling below the **temple** on NE edge of the summit. A wooden stepped path leads down N from here allowing the sure-footed to admire the views while descending. ▶ The wooden steps end at around 1250m, where a well worn path continues down the hillside. After 200m this delves

This section of the path is the Chemin des Chevres or Goat Path.

into a canopy of small deciduous trees. Here take a left branch signposted to Col de Ceyssat. You emerge at a clearing where a **red stone cairn** has a drinking water source. Another signpost points left towards the parking area through a clearing where views are gained. After 50m take the left hand of two forks, heading very gradually down and eventually swinging round the north side of the mountain to return to the upper *auberge* by the **car park**.

Statue of Eugene Renaux on the summit of Puy de Dôme

WALK 17
Puys Lassolas and de la Vache

Start/Finish	Car park 4km NE along the D5 from the D5/N89 junction
Distance	4km
Total Ascent	200m
Difficulty	2
Time	1hr 30mins
Highest Point	1187m
Map	IGN 1:25,000 Sheet 2531ET *Chaîne des Puys*
Public Transport	Buses run along the N89 from Clermont
Parking	Park in the parking area off the D5 close to the junction with the N89 from Clermont

These distinctive semi-circular and modest sized peaks provide an unmissable short outing on one of the Auvergne's most photogenic routes. The Martian-like red summit ridge between Lassolas and Vache not only rewards hikers with expansive views of the puys range, but also with an up close glimpse of twin Strombolian volcanoes.

The Lassolas and Puy de la Vache are the youngest volcanoes in the chain at a mere 8,500 years old. They resulted from a single eruption and their unusual red colour is a result of the extreme heat oxidising the black lava rock. The ancient explosion appears to have blown off the sides of both peaks like America's Mount St Helens – but in fact the lava flow created a sort of landslide to form the steep semi-circular craters of the hills. This route has much to recommend it in the late afternoon or early evening when the colours of the red rocks and verdant forests on the lower slopes are given a spectacular glow by the sun.

The starting point is 4km NE along the D5 from the major N89 road, which goes from Clermont to Rochefort-Montagne. The **car park** spans both sides of the road. Take the path leaving from the W side which follows the road for a short distance before veering right into the forest. After approximately 500m the path passes a left turn marked to the Château du Montlosier, and shortly afterwards there is a right turn which you also ignore. Carry

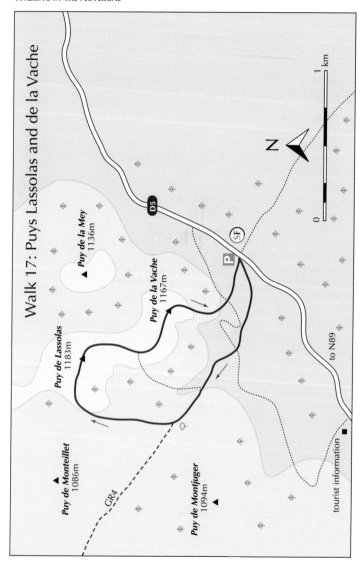

Walk 17: Puys Lassolas and de la Vache

Puy de la Mey
1136m

Puy de la Vache
1167m

Puy de Lassolas
1183m

Puy de Monteillet
1086m

Puy de Montjuger
1094m

GR4

D5

SF

P

N

tourist information

to N89

0   1 km

on to a clearing where there is another right turn. Ignore this as well and continue until a third right turn marked with a red and white marker. To the left of this is an obvious umbrella-shaped huge beech tree. Take this path right dropping into a small trough before climbing up a wide red volcanic scree path. This continues steeply, and a little awkwardly, to the summit of **Puy Lassolas**.

Follow the edge of the semicircular crater over the summit, which has an open outlook and a Martian atmosphere. ▶ At the E side of the Lassolas summit there is a wooden post where a path descends on a river of red scree, which proves pleasant to walk on and leads down to a col in between the two puys, where five paths meet. There is a small copper coloured plate on a tree here which marks the direction of the two summits. The path straight ahead uphill leads to the summit of **Puy de la Vache**, where some twisted large volcanic rocks are strewn. The summit of Vache is gained with considerably more ease than Lassolas.

Descend the Vache by the obvious log steps, ignoring a path which comes off to the right. When the path

The nearby Lake Aydat was formed by the lava flow from the explosion of twin volcanoes Lassolas and Vache.

The volcanic landscape of Puy de la Vache

becomes more gradual follow a more distinct path for 50m which leads into a clearing where there is a noticeboard about vulcanology. Here the continuation of the path is found to your left and leads back to the **parking area**.

The **headquarters** of the Parc Naturel Régional des Volcans d'Auvergne can be found 2km along the D5 SW from the parking area. The administrative buildings for the park are housed in the 18th century Château de Montlosier. There is an interesting visitor centre here which shows films about the area and where maps can be purchased.

WALK 18
Around Orcival

Start/Finish	St Bonnet près Orcival on D27 accessed from N89
Distance	11.5km
Total Ascent	330m
Difficulty	2
Time	3hrs 15mins
Highest Point	1050m
Map	IGN 1:25,000 Sheet 2531ET *Chaîne des Puys*
Public Transport	Nearest transport by bus to Rochefort-Montagne
Parking	In front of St Bonnet church

Orcival is an exceptionally pretty 12th century village which nestles, hidden from view, in the vertiginous Sioulot valley. The village also makes an extremely convenient base from which to explore both the Dôme and Dore areas, positioned between the two mini-ranges and providing varied and popular eating and sleeping options.

This walk approaches Orcival from its attractive neighbour of St Bonnet, allowing hikers to explore open pasture on good tracks, pass a château, chapel and two churches while savouring panoramic views of the Chaîne des Puys to the north and the Sancy massif to the south.

Park at the car park in front of the St Bonnet village **church**. Strike up the road out of the village, passing the town hall on your right. After 100m take a path which branches off left, marked with a green arrow. This joins another road where you again turn left. A further 50m along the road is joined by the D216 to Rochefort.

The Puys stretch across the horizon near Orcival

Take a track opposite, heading uphill past a small disused **quarry** on your right, to soon gain a plateau and rewarding views of the Châine des Puys. ▶ The track leads past a beautiful old stone cross on your left and an ugly pylon on your right, then meets a tarmac road coming from the **Château de Cordés**, which is visible from here. Head through the small settlement of **La Croix**, where a signed path left points up to the Virgin's Chapel. The chapel – with its crypt and spring – is kept locked. From the chapel descend on a surfaced track then take minor roads to reach the centre of **Orcival**.

The forested hill 1.5km ahead of you is the Gravenoire.

NOTRE DAME D'ORCIVAL

Orcival village was founded by the Chaise-Dieu monks in the 12th century and is one of the several French starting points for pilgrims on the Camino. The 12th century basilica at Orcival required the diversion of the local river

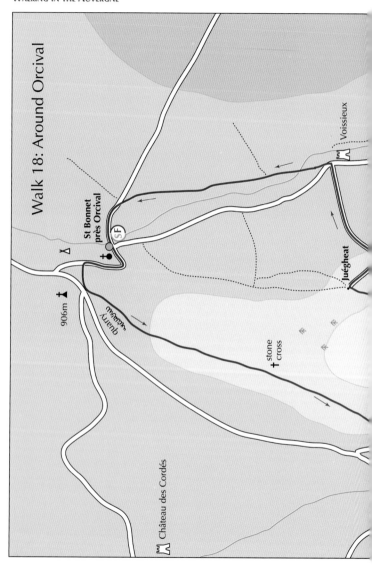

Walk 18: Around Orcival

St Bonnet
près Orcival

SF

906m

quarry

Voissieux

Juegheat

stone
cross

Château des Cordés

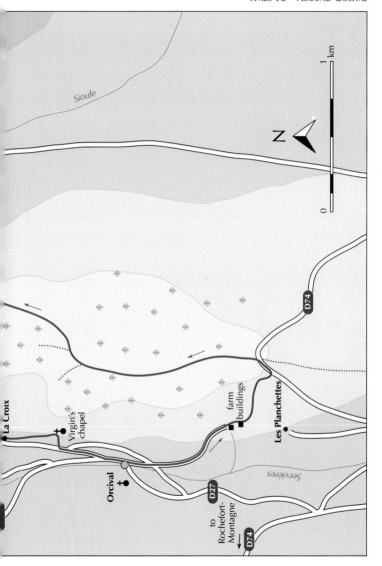

Sioule

N

1 km

0

D74

La Croix

Virgin's
chapel

farm
buildings

Les Planchettes

Orcival

Servières

D27

to
Rochefort-
Montagne

D74

113

and a restructuring of part of the mountainside in order to be built. The master builder was said to have thrown his hammer from the nearby Virgin's Tomb, vowing to build the church on the very spot where it landed.

The basilica contains a famous 10th century statue of the Virgin Mary with a very grown-up looking Jesus on her knee. This has been worshipped since the 6th century, when pilgrims started the tradition on the Feast of the Assumption of a procession carrying the original statue through the streets. The original statue was destroyed by Norman invaders in the 9th century and this replacement was made from wood burnished with silver and gold. The procession continues to this day. It is also said that rays of the midday sun on August 15th – the Assumption – hit the statue on its resting place in the basilica and enshrine the Virgin and Son in a blaze of light.

The village of Orcival and its basilica

Leave Orcival by the road to the left of the water fountain in front of the **basilica**, passing a tourist information building. After 150m meet a crossroads with the main road. Go straight across, following signs to Lac de Serviéres. In 200m take a left fork heading to **farm buildings**, where a spring is marked on the IGN map. From the farm the hill noticeably steepens. The track becomes unsurfaced but well walked. On reaching the

D74 turn left for 100m up to the brow of the hill where the first track left signposted La Croix is taken, leading into mixed deciduous and pine woodland. Head straight across a track crossroads and reach a T junction with a makeshift bench. Go right here down a less worn footpath. After only 100m take the more worn right hand fork down the hill. At another fork bear right and continue until the surfaced road above **Juégheat** is reached. Stay right on the main road here and follow it down the hill to **Voisseaux**. ▶ On reaching a crossroads in Voisseaux take the right-most of three tracks, but only for a few metres, then take a path immediately left, following blue markers. Take care with route-finding here. You should reach the **river Sioule** in no more than 100m. The path now bends N, heading briefly downstream before crossing a bridge by a barn.

A deviation can be made to the château up to the right.

Continue to follow the good farm track parallel to the river until a left on a road leads back across the river Sioule to enter St Bonnet, where a house covered in cycling awards from the 1920s and 1930s can be spotted.

WALK 19
Puy des Gouttes

Start/Finish	Parking area 500m E of D559/D941 roundabout
Distance	6km
Total Ascent	220m
Difficulty	2
Time	1hr 45mins
Highest Point	1134m
Map	IGN 1:25,000 Sheet 2531ET *Châine des Puys*

The route presents hikers with a picturesque and short excursion which showcases another of the area's pristine volcanoes, taking in the flanks of the volcanic Puy des Gouttes. The arcing grassy ridges also give views of the neighbouring Puy Chopine.

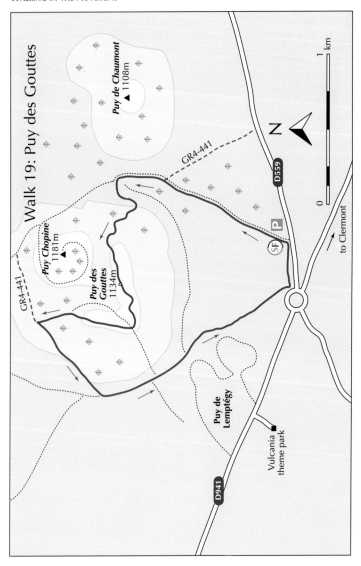

Walk 19: Puy des Gouttes

Puy de Chaumont
▲ 1108m

GR4-441

N

D559

to Clermont

km
0   1

GR4-441

Puy Chopine
▲ 1181m

Puy des
Gouttes
1134m

SF

P

GR4-441

Puy de
Lemptégy

D941

Vulcania
theme park

The **parking area** is 500m E of the roundabout of the **D559** and **D941**. Park on the volcano (N) side of the road. Head N up the wide level forest track from the back of the parking area. After 1km the **GR4-441** track joins from the right. A further 150m brings you to where a forest track branches off right. Ignore this, staying on the main track for a further 20m, where a wooden stile over a fence to the left should be taken. A grassy path leads across a short clearing into a forest. This is marked with the standard red and white GR trail markers and bends left for 100m before turning back right. Shortly after this there is another fork. Follow the marked path rightwards and briefly downhill before the real ascent commences.

Gaining height out of the woods a collection of puys can be seen, all looking like a set of suet puddings. The word 'puy' is specific to the Auvergne region. It comes from the Latin word *podium*, meaning mound.

The wooded top of Puy Chopine from Walk 19

Puy des Gouttes is a small conical volcano of a type known as a cinder or scoria cone. The word scoria comes form the Greek for rust and aptly describes the reddish hue of some of the volcanic matter in the region. Neighbouring Puy Chopine is actually formed from a different trachyte rock.

To the left down the hillside the scar of the Volcan de Lemptégy mine museum can be seen.

Follow the crest of **Puy des Gouttes**, with easy walking on a beautiful ridge to the summit. Only one path leaves the highest spot. Follow this gently round to a second summit. ◄

After having swung round N the GR trail comes off right but stay on the ridge crest path to the gain a third rise. ◄

To the right lies the forested higher summit of Puy Chopine.

Having passed over the third rise the path descends fairly steeply to the left of a fence. After 100m enter woods by way of a wooden stile. Continue following the marked path down until it intersects a wide woodland path, where you turn left. After 600m this becomes a dirt track and reaches a T junction with a gravel path. Take a left here. When this track bends sharply right follow another track leading straight on which becomes grassy and full of meadow flowers, eventually leading back to the **parking area**.

WALK 20

The Crater of Puy Pariou

Start/Finish	Parking area off D941 Clermont–Pontgibaud road nr Orcines
Distance	6.5km
Total Ascent	230m
Difficulty	1
Time	2hrs
Highest Point	1209m
Map	IGN 1:25,000 Sheet 2531ET *Chaîne des Puys*

The Puy Pariou is an attractive volcanic summit to explore due to the simplicity of access, easy ascent and deforested crater rim. It boasts a perfect Christmas pudding shape and a contrasting 100m deep circular hollow in its crater. It is justifiably popular with children and adults alike, as it is easy to imagine its grassy depression bubbling with fiery molten magma.

The Pariou is an example of the Maars type of volcano, where fluid magma met water and caused a hydromagnetic reaction. A tour of the crater's rim gives spectacular 360° views of the Châine des Puys area. Nearby Orcines has several restaurants, two auberges, gîtes and a pleasant campsite.

From the **parking area**, where you'll find La Fontaine du Berger, a drinking water fountain, follow yellow signs to cross the main road and pick up the path going right-wards. Here a gravelly track is crossed to continue on a yellow marked footpath. Cross beneath power lines to get to a junction of paths.

Continue straight on to 'Pariou Sud Est'. Swinging round the conical mountain you emerge from the forest into a first clearing gaining views of Puy de Côme. The path continues to curve around the mountain and the famous sight of the Puy de Dôme rears its massive north side. Passing through a second clearing, ignore a

Fighting erosion: gangplanks on Pariou with the Puy de Dôme behind

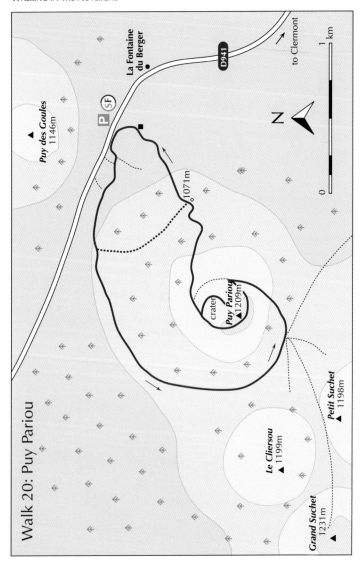

Walk 20: Puy Pariou

path branching off right to **Le Cliersou**. Ascend to a **col** with extensive vistas.

> From the col and crater rim there are good **views of Clermont-Ferrand** – the impressive capital city of the *département*. It is easy to make out the huge black cathedral in the city centre. The 13th century Cathédrale Notre-Dame was crafted from the dark lava stone of slopes at nearby Volvic and its sombre colour gives the building a rather menacing guise.

From the col a clear wooden staircase on your left appears. Take this to ascend to the crater's edge. Going clockwise will take you up to the highest point of the rim.

> The **depression of the crater** is visible but difficult to photograph. For those intrepid enough, a path curls down into the crater where a few cairns are the only sights – you will have to imagine the fiery inferno of lava eruptions for yourself. Strolling around the rim gives ample opportunity to marvel at the dozens of perfect domes scattering the landscape.

Opposite the point you emerged onto the crater rim is a descent path. This contrasts starkly with the ascent route, as it is a simple narrow dirt path heading steeply down through woods. After 600m, at the **1071m spot height**, there is the option of taking a path down to the right which has a yellow 'x' to denote it is not a waymarked route. It is steeper but faster than the yellow marked PR route, which should be taken if knees are feeling fragile. Assuming the first option is chosen, at a T junction turn left and follow a wide grassy path back under the power line. After 100m a wooden kissing gate on the right gives access to another pleasant grassy path which leaves the main track. This passes to the left of a grass-roofed stone **building**. A further 80m along, go through a second kissing gate and follow the path through brush to meet the road in 60m. This brings you out opposite the **parking area** where you started.

WALK 21

The Water of Volvic

Start/Finish	Volvic Source's free visitor centre
Distance	5km (15km for longer circuit)
Ascent	140m (550m)
Difficulty	1 (longer circuit 3)
Time	1hr 30min (longer circuit 5hrs)
Highest Point	674m (754m)
Map	IGN 1:25,000 Sheet 2531ET *Châine des Puys*
Public Transport	Train to Volvic station followed by a signed 2.5km walk on paths to reach the Sources car park
Parking	Free parking at start

Two decent hiking circuits can be made, taking in sights around the famous mineral water town of Volvic. Starting at the source of Volvic water, some moments should be taken to see the somewhat quirky neon-lit gushing pool which brings water from a spring down to be bottled. Also at the start of the route is the Volvic company's free visitor centre, which features a superb film about the Puys and a thirst-quenching tasting room!

The route allows for a trundle up to the Notre Dame de la Garde statue, which overlooks Volvic and provides readers an opportunity to copy the local photo tradition of impersonating her strange stance. The striking hill-top fortress of Tournoël gives another viewpoint and also marks where this route divides: the shorter main route befits those hikers seeking an easy stroll, while the longer extension is suited to hikers strong enough for a more protracted ramble to the Enval gorges and waterfalls.

From the bottom of the **parking area** go left along a small tarmac road, passing signs for a forest theatre.

The building opposite the car park with a plaque and a viewing window allows visitors to peep into the mouth of **the Goulet tunnel** – the source of Volvic mineral water. The tunnel from this spring is 700m long, 70m deep and flows at a rate of 170 litres per second and has served local communities,

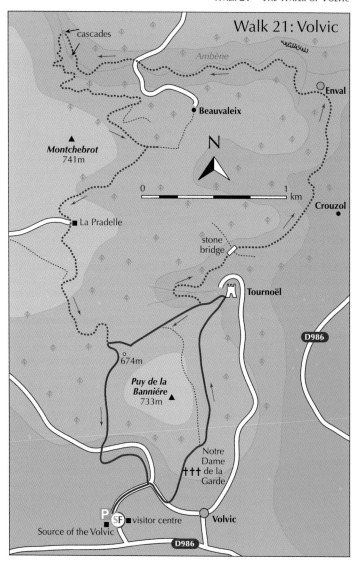

Walk 21: Volvic

cascades

Ambène

○ **Enval**

● **Beauvaleix**

N

▲ *Montchebrot*
741m

0   1
          km

Crouzol ●

■ La Pradelle

stone
bridge ▱

Tournoël ♜ **Tournoël**

D986

○ 674m

*Puy de la
Banniére*
733m ▲

Notre
Dame
de la
Garde
†††

P **SF** ■ visitor centre

Volvic

Source of the Volvic

D986

as well as the drinks company, since it was dug in 1927. The water goes on from here the short distance to the Chancet plants in town to be bottled.

The Volvic spring is fed from the slopes of the Puy de Nugére, where rainfall is filtered through layers of ashy volcanic stone. This is filled with tiny pores which naturally filter and add minerals to the water.

Peering at the source of Volvic water

After 200m turn right at a junction with another small road then take a track left after a further 70m. Follow the signpost to the Château du Tournoël. There is a stone tablet with a map on it marking further destinations. The path from here rises steeply to reach the three impressive **crosses** which overlook Volvic. A further 75m will bring you to the 150-year-old huge brooding statue of **Notre Dame de la Garde**, where a bench near the small chapel allows weary walkers to contemplate the vast views.

> The **worship of the Virgin Mary** is a traditional theme of religion in the Auvergne. These statues were erected by popular demand in the 19th century on high ground to watch over the neighbouring villages and were often teamed with crosses. The Notre-Dame de la Garde was put in place on the slopes of Puy de la Bannière in 1861 and was the work of students at the Volvic school of architecture.

At a T junction after the statue follow the main path right, with le Tournoël marked as 1.2km away. Ignore a further sign going left to Tournoël and go straight on, following red waymarkers.

> Hidden from view on the approach, the **Tournoël château** comes as a surprise. Tournoël was built in the 10th century but was destroyed by Phillippe Auguste in 1213 and was rebuilt and fortified in the 14th century.

For the main, shorter route back from Tournoël follow the red markers left along a wide rising track through the forest to a clearing, ignore smaller paths branching off to both your left and right and pass directly over a col at the 674m spot height. Head steeply downhill on a good path until reaching the road and turn left. A path in the Volvic reserve on the S side of the road continues for 500m until the start of the route is joined and retraced back to the car park.

The three crosses
overlooking Volvic

Extension: Gorges and Cascades of the Ambène river

For the longer route, join the surfaced road on its last bend
at Tournoël. Head downhill for only 25m until a small
path can be found on your left heading W, downhill. This
path is tricky to find. Once joined the route eventually
swings round a forested catchment area, crossing two
streams and descending gradually for another 500m to
a large stone **bridge** covered in ivy which is also marked
on the IGN map.

After the bridge the path splits. Go straight on up a small narrow path swinging right and climbing through the forest. Continue uphill gradually for 450m, where the path is joined by another from the left and starts to descend. After a further 100m it is joined by yet another path, this time from the right, and crosses a little stone bridge. Pass around a streambed and reach a hairpin where the left hand of two ways is taken gradually uphill. At a further hairpin three options are to be discovered, take the middle of these marked 'Apache Way'. Following this path, the cliffs of the Ambène river gorge come briefly into view.

After 400m cross a wooden bridge and 150m more will lead you to an orientation table and at last some excellent views over **Enval** to the Monts du Forez and Bourbonnaise. ▶ Continue to where the path joins the river bank at a bench and keep following the Apache Indian signs. A wooden bridge marked '9 Mai' is eventually traversed. Turn left and follow the river up on the right hand bank until intersecting a road with a picnic bench which leads to Beauvaleix. Cross the road and follow a sign to the cascades on a path which is not marked on the IGN maps. This path stays right of the river, climbing briefly out of the gorge.

Take care here as the gorges are steep-sided.

After 600m reach a bridge where a 10 minute detour to the first set of **cascades**, the misnamed Grand Girand, can theoretically be taken. However, these falls are both difficult and dangerous to access and not really worth the effort. Unless some comprehensive path restructuring has been done since our visit, head upstream to the more impressive upper falls – the Petit Girand. ▶ Beyond the upper falls continue to follow yellow Apache and Cascades Loop signs as the path climbs up left, leaving the river behind, and swings monstrously round the hillside through oak and beech woods. The signposted route continues circuitously and tiringly up endless switchbacks and undulations not marked on the IGN map towards the hamlet of **Beauvaleix**. ▶ After what seems an eternity a track is met. Turn left on this going gradually downhill towards Beauvaleix, which soon comes into view.

The largest cascade on the Ambène was called 'The End of the World' in a work by the French author Maupassant.

The wooded terrain here is extremely disorientating and a degree of faith is required.

At an open area before Beauvaleix our track is joined by a track from the right. Double back along this. A further 250m brings you to a fork just after a green way-marker on a stone embedded in the track. Take the right hand option uphill, following a small power line. After a sharp bend left continue straight on at a junction to pass **la Pradelle**, a solitary but very large house, to your left. At a fork 200m after Pradelle turn right through brush and open land to join the GR 441 trail 50m later. Follow this and its red and white markers left, winding down to an open col (674m) where a small right hand path cuts off the corner and joins the steep descent of the primary route back to the **Source of the Volvic**.

THE MONTS DORE

Evening by the Grande Cascade (Walk 25)

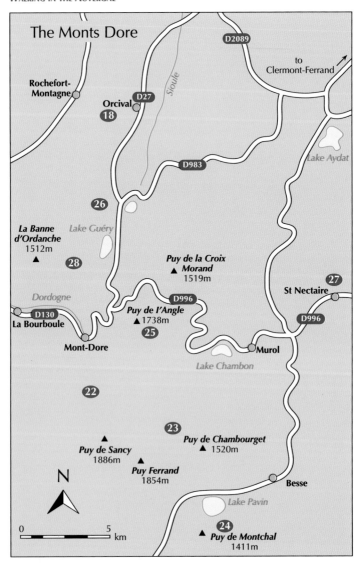

The Monts Dore

INTRODUCTION

Great picnic views: Sancy ridge (Walk 22)

The Monts Dore offer a range of exceptional hiking amid volcanic scenery dominated by the alluring, vertiginous Puy de Sancy – at 1885m the highest mountain in central France. The area, also known as the Massif du Sancy, borders the Châine des Puys and has an uncanny knack of providing superb routes which leave a lasting impression. The finest of these is the colossal Puy de Sancy horseshoe, arguably one of the best hikes in France.

That said, it is worth exploring further afield. The area's other principal peaks of Puy Ferrand and the Banne d'Ordanche give enticing objectives, along with the gargantuan rock edifices of the Sanadoire and Tuiliéres and the volcanic crater lake of Pavin. The sublime Grande Cascade – the highest waterfall in the Auvergne – should not be missed and is incorporated into Walks 22 (the Puy de Sancy horseshoe) and 25. The topography of the Monts Dore favours multi-peak ridge crest link-ups and while the valleys are more populated than those of the Monts du Cantal, these are quickly exchanged for tremendous mountain terrain.

The namesake spa town of Mont-Dore is a somewhat inevitable honeypot crammed into the start of the Dordogne valley at the foot of the Sancy massif. It is vibrant, blessed with excellent hotels, restaurants and shops, and surprisingly adds colour to the views from the walks which climb above it.

As the Monts Dore area adjoins the Châine des Puys, it is worth considering locations listed in the previous chapter which prove convenient points of access to both areas. The Sancy Massif boasts a decent-sized ski area in winter which links Mont-Dore with the Station de Super-Besse and a third smaller resort at Chastreix. Together these offer various types of summer accommodation. The spa town of Mont-Dore has a high quality campsite situated close to the centre and is a good option for those using public transport. Additionally it offers a full spectrum of accommodation, from hostels to high class hotels. In summer the area is becoming more popular for mountain bikers and further east, Lac Chambon is popular with watersports enthusiasts. Further along the Couze Chambon valley, those wanting to escape the high summits will enjoy discovering villages such as Murol, with its clifftop castle, and the spa town of St Nectaire with its imposing church and ancient dolmen.

As also mentioned in the preceding chapter, the Monts Dore and Châine des Puys can be visited from the same base and both Orcival and the nearby village of St Bonnet are recommended for this purpose. For those basing themselves further south there are several good choices. The attractive towns of Besse and La Bourboule give easy access to these walks with plenty of good facilities and the village of Murat-le-Quaire is a quieter option.

WALK 22

The Grand Horseshoe: Puy de Sancy from Mont-Dore

Start/Finish	Mont-Dore funicular station on W side of town centre (Station du Mont-Dore for shorter walk)
Distance	16.5km (shorter walk 7 km)
Total Ascent	1050m (shorter walk 570m)
Difficulty	3 (shorter walk 2)
Time	6hrs (shorter walk 3hrs 15mins)
Highest Point	1885m
Map	IGN 1:25,000 Sheet 2432ET *Massif du Sancy*
Public Transport	Train to Mont-Dore from Clermont-Ferrand
Parking	Free parking area close to the funicular station

At a height of 1885m, Puy de Sancy boasts the honour of being the highest peak in both the Auvergne and indeed the whole Massif Central. The peak itself is eminently impressive, with formidable spiky-looking ridges, twisting, folded valleys and precipitous N and S faces. Our main route amply rewards those prepared to expend a little more energy and time with one of the finest hiking horseshoes, not only in the Auvergne, but in France. Although purists may recoil at the proliferation of skiing accoutrements adorning Sancy's northern flank, by ascending the longer option described here the hiker can, for the majority of the route, be blissfully unaware of the human impact on the mountain. There is also a greater chance of solitude on the long route, until reaching the summit area which is, admittedly, fairly hectic by Auvergne standards (at least when the ski-lift is open), but consoles nonetheless with impressive views that, on good days and with super-hero vision, extend as far as Mont Blanc to the east.

Peace is soon restored on leaving the summit area for the second half of the horseshoe and the huge circuit incorporates the extremely impressive Grande Cascade (at 32m the highest waterfall in the Auvergne) as its finale. On hot days hikers can be found clambering behind the falls and cooling down in its spray with rainbows bursting out in every direction. It is on the verdant flanks of the Sancy that two streams named the Dore and the Dogne tumble down the steep hillsides to merge and form the mighty Dordogne River. Supposedly Sancy is the domain of chamois, mouflon and marmots, but these tend to hide in peak season.

133

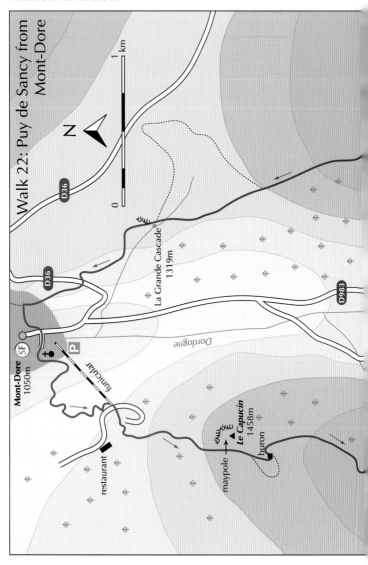

Walk 22: Puy de Sancy from Mont-Dore

N

0 1 km

D36

D36

D983

Mont-Dore 1050m

SF

P

funicular

restaurant

La Grande Cascade 1319m

Dordogne

maypole

Le Capucin 1458m

buron

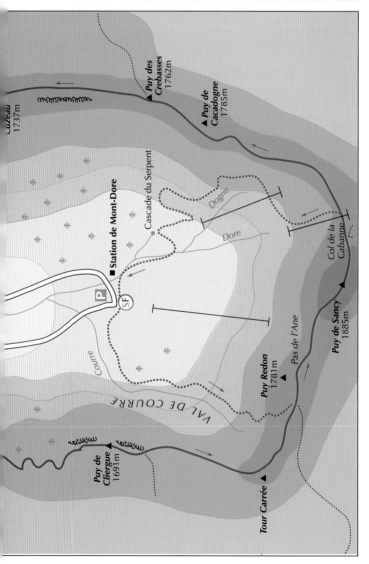

Puy des Crebasses 1762m

Puy de Cacadogne 1785m

...eau 1737m

Cascade du Serpent

Dogne

Dore

Station de Mont-Dore

Col de la Cabanne

Puy de Sancy 1885m

Pas de l'Ane

Puy Redon 1781m

VAL DE COURRE

Courre

Puy de Cliergue 1691m

Tour Carrée

135

If you want to reach the summit of Puy de Sancy more quickly you can take an alternative shorter route up the Courre valley, where a little seclusion from the paraphernalia of the Sancy ski area can be had. This is described below. The descent route is, however, on an ugly ski track under various lifts. A sensible even quicker option perhaps might be to ascend the cable car and the short distance to the summit then return via the Courre valley in around 1hr 10min.

Across the river on the SW side of Mont-Dore there is a convenient free parking area close to the **funicular** station (public toilets) where there is also a small church.

The quaint **funicular** is the oldest electric mountain railway in France: it has taken tourists up to the Salon du Capucin station at 1245m since 1898, and is an option for those wishing to cut out the initial steep ascent, deducting 180m of climbing. The cable car and funicular are both open every day from June to September for walkers from 9am to 6pm. A one way ticket for both costs €8 at the time of writing.

Several shorter walking options can be designed using the funicular and/or the cable car which leads from Station du Mont-Dore up to just below the Pas de l'Ane: see also the shorter circuit from Station du Mont-Dore described below.

From the small **church** beneath the funicular station take the road away from the river for 50m or so. As the road begins to bend look out for the yellow walking sign to 'Station du Mont-Dore and Le Capucin'. Turn left up this initially surfaced track, passing between two buildings to enter woods and climb steeply. A much wider track is soon intersected: turn right on this, but after only 30m and before reaching a bench take a left uphill on a wide path still in the forest. This path gradually leads to the upper funicular station with its parking area and **restaurant**. Opposite the entrance to the funicular station, a narrower path heads straight on and passes beneath the zip wires of an adventure playground. Take this and emerge on tarmac south of a large restaurant and parking area. At a junction with another track turn left, following the signpost to Le Capucin. A little further on, the shadowy crags of Le Capucin come into view for the first time: this is the large rocky mound with a maypole on top visible from Mont-Dore.

The track passes W of the summit of **Le Capucin**. Look out for a path to the left which enables you to cut off a dog leg and brings you back to the original route at a **buron**, where a fence is crossed by a metal stile. ▶ Ignore a path up left to the tempting summit of Le Capucin, unless of tireless energy and wanting to bag an extra summit with a 20 minute detour. Head straight on along the grassy path gradually uphill, with Puy de Cliergue visible ahead. The path steepens, navigating a large rock buttress after which at a path junction, and where a ruin can be seen, our route heads left signed to Puy de Sancy. **Puy de Cliergue**'s 1691m summit is marked with a wooden post and plaque. From here the path advances on the left of

The forest clears here and good views of the distant square rocky summit of Banne d'Ordanche to your rear NNW are gained.

Mont-Dore is down there somewhere: on the Sancy ridge

a fence with dramatic drops to your left. The horseshoe arcs east at **Tour Carrée** and winds sublimely and easily around various rocky outcrops on the narrow ridge. ◄ A small section of stone steps overcomes a buttress, while a small descent to the **Pas de l'Ane** intervenes before the erosion-preserving wooden steps to the absolute top of Sancy commence, and where the path from the cable car station is met.

The **summit** (1885m) has a large orientation table with 360° views of the Massif Central. From the top take a clear path SE, descending steeply to the **Col de la Cabanne**: this proves the most awkward hiking of the whole route, but is short-lived. When this path splits take the left option, descending E. After 300m pass a turnoff left which goes straight back to Mont-Dore (avoid the temptation to take this, you have done the bulk of the hard work and the reward of the Grande Cascade beckons). Head straight on working gradually uphill, contouring round **Puy de Cacadogne** and gaining stunning views of the Chaudefour valley to your right. At the summit of **Puy des Crebasses** the path forks, right heads to the Chaudefour valley while we take the left fork. ◄ You

make one final ascent to the **Roc de Cuzeau** summit and though you may be weary now, be consoled, it is all free-wheeling from here, with gradual easy hiking on good paths. From the summit the route doubles back right and leaves the ridge crest to zigzag down, bringing you to a wide shoulder with a cairn. Here, traverse left, as if heading back towards Le Capucin on the other side of the valley. This circuitous route brings you back to the crest but avoids the steepest and most eroded section of the path.

After 300m follow a signed route to the Grande Cascade on a fainter path staying with the ridge crest. A further 500m brings you to a wooden stile, which is crossed. Shortly above the tree-line the path veers into the catchment area of the river where the impressive **Grande Cascade** is located. The path splits up here but all options appear to lead to the same place at the left side of the falls, where metal steps aid your descent.

The **impressive waterfall** is very pretty and has a 32m drop. Those passing on hot days may join the French water nymphs and take advantage of one of nature's best cooling showers.

Cooling off in the Grande Cascade

At the foot of the waterfall cross a tiny wooden bridge and take the only descending path steeply through the forest for 1km. On nearing the **D36** road switch back left for 60m, ignoring a path going right. Cross the road and turn right where a yellow sign marks the Chemin de Melchi-Rose path heading back right. This traverses the hillside above Mont-Dore. There are surprisingly few views of Mont-Dore itself and the path proves pleasant here. After 700m a path leads left down the hill straight into the centre of **Mont-Dore**. Take this to emerge at some stone steps very close to the thermal baths in the centre of the town. From here head straight across the pedestrianised area to find the **parking area** and funicular station across the bridge. Treat yourself to a hearty meal and a pat on the back for completing such a grand walk.

Shorter circuit from Station du Mont-Dore

Start from the right hand corner of the large car park at the top of the dead-end Station du Mont-Dore road. From here an obvious path marked with red and white markers leads up under the furthest chairlift to the right. This swings into the pleasant **Val de Courre**. The path heads up to the top of the lift and then follows the stream uphill on well-trodden ground which steepens towards the head of the valley.

The route gains the ridge at the col between **Puy Redon** and **Tour Carreé** where there is a sign pointing left to Puy de Sancy on a clear path. This heads behind Puy Redon then is joined by a path from the cable car at **Pas de l'Ane**. The last section to **Sancy's summit** is gained by way of wooden steps.

Follow the path off the E side of the summit which leads fairly steeply down to the **Col de la Cabanne**. Here there is an obvious track going down from the col. This is a tedious but easy descent leading all the way back under another chairlift and eventually to the car park. A short deviation can be made just after the bottom of the highest chairlift to visit the Dore waterfall. This is nowhere near as impressive as the Grande Cascade visited on the main route.

Looking towards the magnificent Sancy massif

WALK 23

Up the Chaudefour Valley to
Puys Sancy and Ferrand

Start/Finish	Chaudefour Valley parking area on the D36 from Besse-en-Chandesse
Distance	13.5km
Total Ascent	900m
Difficulty	3
Time	5hrs
Highest Point	1885m
Map	IGN 1:25,000 Sheet 2432ET Massif du Sancy

The spectacular Chaudefour lays claim to be the Auvergne's wildest valley. Although this would be difficult to believe on a sunny summer's day when the valley floor is teeming with walkers, Chaudefour remains unspoilt and its volcanic rock spires and abundant plants and wildlife make it a hiking heaven. After the Sancy and Ferrand had been formed by volcanoes, a glacier carved out the Chaudefour valley leaving the lava plug needles of the Dent de la Rancune and Crête de Coq as evidence of erstwhile eruptions. Now deemed a nature reserve, the valley allows no dogs, bikes or camping and the spiky rocks shelter birds such a peregrine falcons, rock swallows and ravens.

From the Chaudefour Valley **parking area** go past the tourist information office in the **Nature Reserve headquarters** (public toilets). Here a single track leads into the Chaudefour valley. Ignore a first right hand spur. After 700m the **Cascade de Pérouse** is well worth a visit and is reached by a 60m deviation to the left from the path. A bridge soon takes hikers over the **River Biche**: continue upstream into the open meadows of the Chaudefour, where an information board and the jagged twin edifices of **La Dent de la Rancune** and the **Crête de la Coq** – the 'Bitter Tooth' and the 'Cock's Comb' – are revealed.

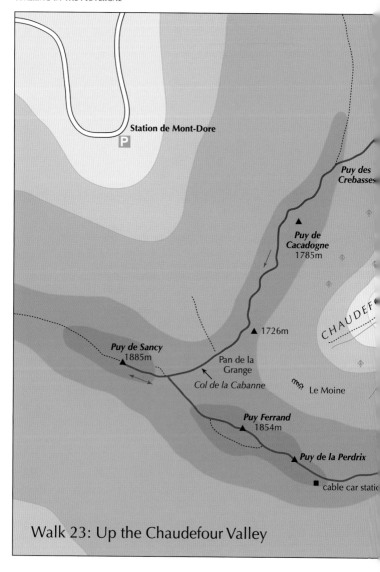

Station de Mont-Dore

Puy des Crebasses

▲ **Puy de Cacadogne**
1785m

▲ 1726m

CHAUDEF

Puy de Sancy
1885m
▲

Pan de la
Grange

Col de la Cabanne

Le Moine

Puy Ferrand
1854m
▲

▲ **Puy de la Perdrix**

■ cable car statio

Walk 23: Up the Chaudefour Valley

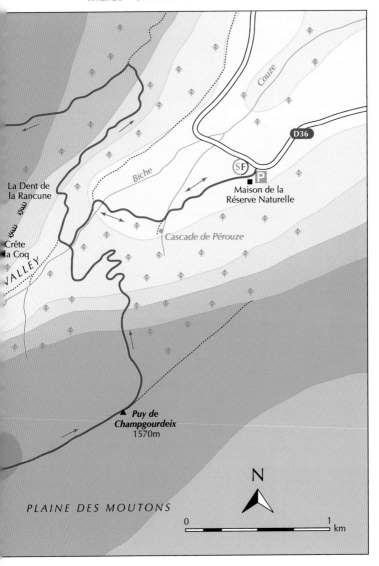

La Dent de
la Rancune

Crête
a Coq

VALLEY

Couze

Biche

D36

SF P

Maison de la
Réserve Naturelle

Cascade de Pérouze

▲ *Puy de*
Champgourdeix
1570m

PLAINE DES MOUTONS

N

0   1
                    km

The Dent de la Rancune and Crête de la Coq in the verdant Chaudefour valley

For those pushed for time, a worthwhile 1hr 'there and back' route is recommended in order to explore the **lower part of the Chaudefour Valley**. By following the route description outbound beyond the bridge across the Biche and into the meadows, walkers will be able to enjoy mouth-watering views and perhaps laze and picnic on the valley floor beneath the famous rock formations having exerted little energy.

The Chaudefour Valley nature reserve could provide a good chance of spotting unusual wildlife if you pick a quiet day. Various animals native to other parts of France have been successfully introduced in the area including mouflon, chamois and marmot.

The mountain at the head of the valley is the Puy Ferrand.

◀ After 200m reach a signpost at a junction of four paths. Here an orange route marked 'Sentier de Liadouze' is taken rightwards, initially on a grassy path which soon leaves the meadows behind and goes through a gate into the woods. A slight descent is made before switchbacks uphill are followed. Here care must be taken to follow the orange markers. Height is gained slowly. One bend provides impressive views of the rock features and the valley floor. Once you've worked up a good sweat, the path emerges from the woods into broom and open pasture. The path here is less distinct, but trend leftwards across the plateau to a junction at a col where there is a small cairn and an orange post. Turn left up the steep wide grassy path. A stile crosses a fence and the route leads up to where a third spiky rock perched on the N face of the Puy Ferrand called le Moine can be seen. The ridge crest becomes more defined.

Close to the summit of the **Puy des Crebasses**, our path is joined by the GR4 route and skirts around the actual peak. ▶ The summit of **Puy de Cacadogne** is skirted on its NW flank. After negotiating the shoulder of this mountain, descend to a col where le Moine needle looks ready to pierce the sky beneath you. The path follows the ridge crest before descending once more to the **Pan de la Grange**, where you will be joined by other hikers trying to reach the summit of the Sancy. Head straight on here in the direction of the Sancy summit, soon reaching the **Col de la Cabanne** at 1785m.

Here the first good views of the Puy de Sancy with its ski station are gained.

> A **deviation to the top of the Sancy** takes 20–30mins and requires a short sharp burst of energy to overcome the 100m of height gain necessary. The Sancy summit provides an orientation table and extensive views.

From the Col de la Cabanne, where a pessimistic sign gives 3hrs back down to the Chaudefour valley (don't worry, this is totally inaccurate), continue on our horseshoe SE on a clear path (not marked on the IGN map) which forks off left to the top of **Puy Ferrand**. From the summit follow another clear path descending a narrow spur of hillside all the way to the col between Ferrand and Puy de la Perdrix, which is identified by the concrete cable car building behind it.

Stay on the most worn upper path on the ridge crest, easily conquering **Puy de la Perdrix**. An initially steep

*The bustling summit
area of Puy de Sancy*

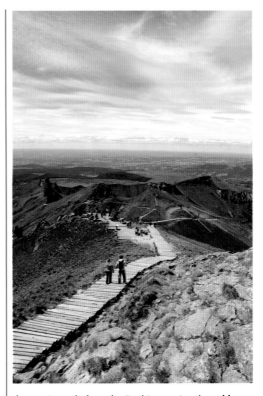

descent is made from the Perdrix, passing the **cable car
station** to your right, then easing to meander pleasantly
downhill, until a gentle potter uphill to cross the summit
of **Puy de Champgourdeix** must be made. After crossing
the level summit area of Champgourdeix (1570m) the
path forks, with our route bearing left (N). Head initially
through broken woodland. The ground steepens and the
path descends into thicker woods. On this section the
route is marked with yellow dots and the path becomes
a little rougher. After a barbed wire fence is crossed, the
descent path returns to the valley floor, crossing a bridge
and rejoining the outbound route at the signpost.

WALK 24

Around Lake Pavin

Start/Finish	Large parking area off the D149 5km from Besse-en-Chandesse
Distance	4km
Total Ascent	100m
Difficulty	1
Time	1hr 20mins
Highest Point	1260m
Map	IGN 1:25,000 Sheet 2432ET *Massif du Sancy*
Public Transport	Bus to Besse from Clermont

Although this area of the Auvergne is famed for its volcanoes and its lakes, many of the latter seem over-developed and unsuitable for tranquil waterside walking. Lake Pavin, although attracting its fair share of visitors, is an exception to this rule. In spite of its accessibility – all facilities including camping and hotels are available in nearby Besse – the lake has no roads along its shoreline and just one lakeside building. On a sunny day Pavin's water gleams temptingly. From above, the lake seems to blink its lovely azure eye at the hiker. Pavin is nestled in the youngest volcanic crater in France. While rambling around the steep-sided tree-lined bowl which hosts the lake, one can imagine the eruption of Puy de Montchal which formed the lake and whose gentle upper slopes can be seen to the right at the highest point of this walk.

Start from the main **parking areas** by the roundabout on the D149 which are signposted clearly for visitors to Lake Pavin. Do not be tempted in peak season to drive further up the road and add to the unnecessary parking chaos created by those wanting to get even closer to the lake.

From the parking areas signs mark the route to the lake. Follow a gravel path from the corner of the car park furthest from the road. This trends gradually uphill below a minor road for 400m until reaching the lakeside at a gift shop, restaurant and **toilets**. ▶

This section of the path gives views rightwards to Puy de Chambourguet and Puy de Serveix across the valley.

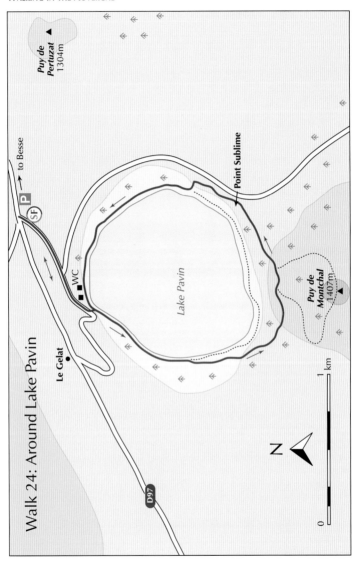

Walk 24: Around Lake Pavin

Puy de Pertuzat 1304m

to Besse

SF

P

WC

Le Gelat

Lake Pavin

Point Sublime

Puy de Montchal 1407m

D97

N

0   1 km

The **boardwalks** at the head of Lake Pavin by the restaurant are popular with picnickers as the crystalline waters provide a stunning backdrop.

Leaky boat moored at Lake Pavin

Here our route goes right along the wide lake shore path, where mainly beech woods give dappled shade on a hot day but rarely become so dense that the lake completely disappears from sight.

Through breaks in the foliage the evidence of the lake's volcanic origin can be seen in the form of **basalt columns** dropping down to the eastern shoreline. The volcanic eruption which formed Lake Pavin took place a mere 6000 years ago and was of the Maar type. Lake Pavin is close to 100m deep, and to put that in perspective, Wast Water, England's deepest lake, is 79m deep.

After 600m on the lake shore look out for a well-walked path splitting off to the right and heading uphill. This can be found just after some small rock buttresses.

149

For those wanting an even **shorter and more level excursion**, the lakeside path can be followed for the whole distance around the lake.

The good right hand path climbs quite steeply and eventually loses sight of the lake down below. The climb ends after approximately 700m, where a popular route coming from the distant Lac Chauvet joins the path from the right. Go left here and ignore another route going right to **Puy de Montchal** which splits off after 50m. The path leads into pine forest for 300m until emerging at the **Point Sublime**, where there is a car park along with spectacular viewpoints of the lake below, nestled in its tree-lined crater. ◄

Looking across the lake further north the higher summits of Puys Paillaret, Perdrix and Ferrand frame the view.

From the top of the path head straight on, continuing just left of the parking area along the lake's crater rim. The path continues straight ahead without crossing the minor road – good picnic spots abound. After 200m take a left-wards path to begin a descent back to the lakeside. After 150m the path seems to double back on itself and the left option signposted with warnings about loose rock is taken. A further 50m along the path turns back rightwards and continues down to the lake. Follow the path for a further 1km to bring you back to the restaurant at the head of the lake. Retrace your steps from here to the **car park**.

WALK 25

Connecting the Cascades of Puy d'Angle

Start/Finish	Prends-toi-Garde at the N side of Mont-Dore
Distance	16km
Total Ascent	930m
Difficulty	3
Time	5hrs 30mins
Highest Point	1738m
Map	IGN 1:25,000 Sheet 2432ET *Massif du Sancy*
Public Transport	Bus and rail to Mont-Dore
Parking	Parking area for the cemetery and short waterfall walk

This long hike is one of the stellar routes of the area, although it does not appear to be an obvious itinerary when glancing at the IGN map. An authors' favourite, two of the most spectacular waterfalls in the Auvergne are coupled with excellent ridge walking and superlative views of all the major summits of the Monts Dore and Dômes including Puy de Sancy and Puy de Dôme. The azure waters of Lake Guery twinkle beneath you and the large town of Mont-Dore is hidden from view for the majority of the route, and when it does appear, it tends to be framed in a picturesque fashion. Even a short section of tarmac trudging cannot detract from the otherwise pristine surroundings and a route which, for the most part, avoids the crowds

To reach the start, from the D996 at the N end of Mont-Dore look out for signs to the Esquiladon campsite and le Queureulidh. Drive past the campsite until reaching the parking area for the cascades and **cemetery**. From here head up the right edge of the graveyard on a surfaced dead-end road. Turn right off this after 500m onto a gravel track heading into a forest. After a short signed detour to the magnificent **Cascade du Queureulih** falls, follow the main track downhill (leftwards). Cross the river by a wooden bridge and after 100m turn right along another track going gradually uphill.

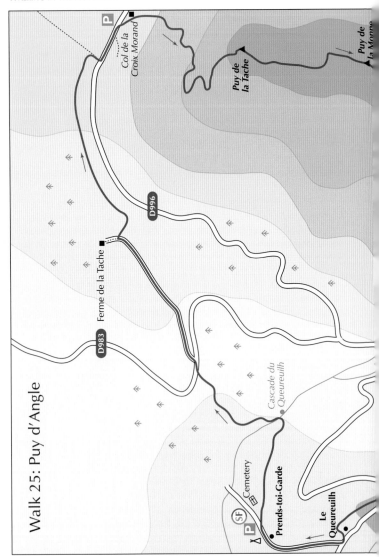

Walk 25: Puy d'Angle

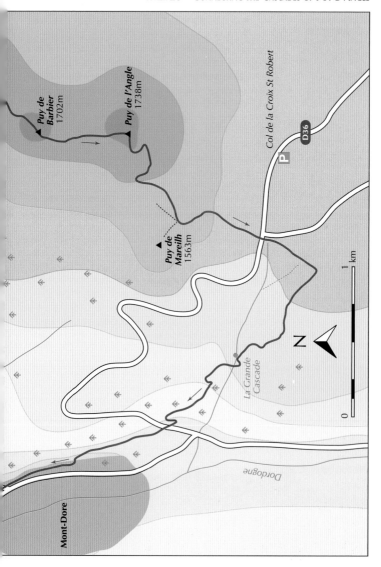

Puy de Barbier 1702m

Puy de l'Angle 1738m

Puy de Mareilh 1563m

Col de la Croix St Robert

D36

P

La Grande Cascade

Dordogne

Mont-Dore

N

1 km

0

153

After 1km the track brings you to the **D983**. Here go left and then immediately right following a surfaced track on the opposite side of the road which leads up to the **Ferme de La Tache** (farm). At a hairpin bend on the track just before the farm come off rightwards on a path with red waymarkers. Pass through a gate in a barbed wire fence. The path is grassy and easy to follow. Before reaching a *buron* it bends left and climbs up towards another section of forest. Cross a fence via metal steps to enter the forest, where the path narrows. This eventually emerges from the forest and two minor streams are forded. Continue on the main path with the **D996** road to the right above you. At a junction by a gate join the main road.

Unfortunately there is no path here and you must walk up the road for 300m to the **Col de la Croix Morand**, where there is a parking area and a restaurant. ◄ At the col take a path on the right of an old concrete building and cross the fence by means of a stile. The path is peaty and may get boggy in bad weather. Zigzag uphill to eventually reach a small shoulder where a left turn is made. Cross a stile to reach a weather station at the summit of **Puy de la Tache** (1629m).

Descend from Tache to a col after which the path splits: peak baggers may want to head left but most sane people will take the right hand option which skirts the

Remember to walk on the left side of the road facing the oncoming traffic.

Crooked cross on Puy d'Angle

summit of **Puy de la Monne**. Continue along the majestic ridge to **Puy de Barbier**, which has a big cairn on its summit. Little height is lost as another col is crossed and the high point of the ridge, **Puy de l'Angle**, is reached. The summit is marked by a cairn.

From the summit head fairly steeply down the most distinct path, passing an oddly bent white cross and over a stile. Follow this peaty and eroded path for 700m until reaching a col, where a small path branches up right to a further summit, **Puy de Mareilh**. Ignore this and cross a wooden stile to continue descending between two fences towards the visible **D36** at the **Col de la Croix St Robert**.

On reaching the road a sign states 3km to Mont-Dore. Go straight ahead on this path. In 60m cross a stile and a stream before the main path swings right, first climbing and then contouring the hillside above the river gorge. Ignore various smaller paths heading left (uphill). The peaty path passes through woodland until a small wooden bridge is seen to the right. Do not cross this but continue veering left uphill here to emerge at a dramatic overlook above cliffs, with superb views of Mont-Dore and Le Capucin, with its maypole summit. A right down some reinforced steps leads to the impressive 32m waterfall of the **Grande Cascade** (the highest in the Auvergne), where on hot days the young and beautiful and old and wrinkly alike shed clothes for natural showers and ambles behind the falls.

At the foot of the waterfall cross a tiny wooden bridge and take the only descending path steeply through the forest for 1km. On nearing the **D36** road switch back left for 60m, ignoring a path going right. Cross the road and turn right where a yellow sign marks the Chemin de Melchi-Rose path heading back right, traversing the hillside above **Mont-Dore**. ▶

There are surprisingly few views of Mont-Dore and the hiking proves pleasant.

The Auvergne is nicknamed the 'water castle of France' due to its many **mineral and thermal springs**. The spa waters at Mont-Dore have reputedly been curing visitors of respiratory problems and rheumatism for over 200 years.

After 700m a path leads left down the hill straight into the centre of Mont-Dore. If you have parked at the cemetery, continue straight ahead with a very small ascent. After 400m a second path descending left into Mont-Dore marked as Chemin de la Chappe also needs to be ignored. Continue on until you reach the **D986** road.

Head right uphill for 300m on this and, just after passing the final houses, take a path marked in green and red which comes off to the left. Descend a few steps to re-enter the forest on a fairly narrow path. This zigzags into **le Queureuilh**, where you meet a minor road. Turn right up this past the campsite and back to the **cemetery**.

WALK 26
The Tuilière and Sanadoire rocks

Start/Finish	Parking area off the D80 4km from the Col de Guéry
Distance	7km
Total Ascent	330m
Difficulty	2 (1 if omitting Sanadoire ridge deviation)
Time	2hrs–2hrs 20mins
Highest Point	1260m
Map	IGN 1:25,000 Sheet 2432ET *Massif du Sancy*

The imposing cliffs of Tuilière and Sanadoire are seen by thousands of tourists each year from the roadside belvedere at the Col de Guéry. However, few venture up close to marvel at the vast basalt towers and mighty columns comprising the two edifices. The rock formations were created by magma 2 million years ago. The lava here was so viscous that it did not spread out but instead rose upwards, creating the marvellous phonolite structures. The Fontsalade valley which was subsequently carved out by glaciers has made the sheer faces of the two rocks appear even more dramatic.

To reach the start of the walk by car, from the Col de Guéry parking area a minor road (D80) is followed for 4km until a rough parking area below the cliffs on the left hand side of the road. There is no public transport access.

From the **parking area** follow the road left for 50m until a path with yellow markers leaves to the right. Take this down into the woods. After 70m, and having crossed the river, turn right at a junction with a track. Look out for a yellow marked path beneath the Sanadoire forking to the left, take this until a sharp right leads to a wooden bridge after 50m. Do not cross the bridge, and so, ignoring the yellow markers, go straight along the path on the E left side of the **Fontsalade river**.

The path soon leaves the river and heads leftwards, uphill, through mixed pine and beech woodland. On reaching the **D80** road turn right and 30m later take a path across the road, starting on a wooden bridge near a small waterworks. Cross a stream and ascend through the forest. After 200m the path joins an old, wide track. Turn

Face off: the Tuiliére and Sanadoire rocks from the Col de Guéry

157

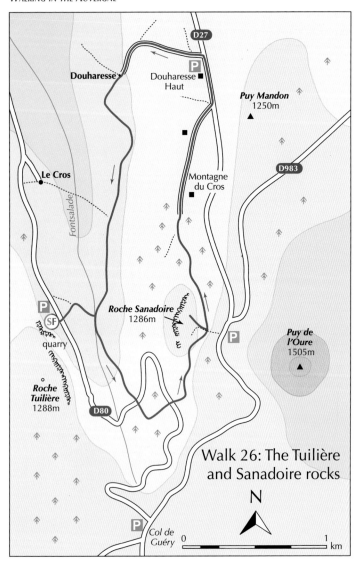

Douharesse

D27

Douharesse
Haut

Puy Mandon
1250m

Le Cros

Fontsalade

D983

Montagne
du Cros

quarry

Roche Sanadoire
1286m

*Puy de
l'Oure*
1505m

*Roche
Tuilière*
1288m

D80

Walk 26: The Tuilière
and Sanadoire rocks

N

Col de
Guéry

0   1
                                    km

left here. After passing a wooden gate the road is crossed once more. The continuation path is easy to spot on the opposite side and traverses the wooded hillside, while the Sanadoire looms darkly through the trees. Eventually the path will lead you to the small col between a roadside viewing area on your right and the top of the **Roche Sanadoire** to your left.

> The **hexagonal columns** of Sanadoire were formed by a complex interaction between fissures in the granite base rock and the cooling lava. This attempted to retreat while the top layer was continuously cooling in the air and being dried and split by the sun.

CLIMBING THE SHOULDER OF THE ROCHE SANADOIRE

The route goes straight on, but a left turn here (marked with a blue 'X') can be made for the intrepid, and provides a deviation to a spectacular shoulder on the ridge of the Sanadoire itself. This is a fantastic viewing point but care must be taken.

A desperately loose and exposed climbers' path does reach the actual summit but this is definitely not recommended. Ascending this is forbidden for hikers, having been deemed extremely dangerous, not merely because of its gradient but for its extremely loose terrain. In omitting this treacherous route you are not missing anything beyond a very precarious dance with death. To get to the much safer ridge-top viewing area turn left at the small col, ignoring the blue 'X'.

The path from the col leads up steeply to the toe of the furthermost buttress of the Sanadoire – ignore a climber's path coming off left here. At the rock wall follow the path rightwards, skirting the cliff on its N side. After 25m the path splits. Do not go left up the gully but traverse gradually through the forest. The path eventually steepens and some stepped grass allows you to reach a small eagle-perch viewpoint area, from which the sheer cliffs drop away dramatically.

This is an excellent vantage point from which to appreciate Roche Tuiliére. This detour is not advised for those without a head for heights, but nevertheless the ascent in no way involves scrambling, merely some steep terrain. Photos taken, retrace your steps to the col.

Roche Tuiliére from La Montagne du Cros

From the col follow the narrow path through the forest downhill. After 350m take the path swinging leftwards which continues straight ahead, marked with a blue 'X'. This brings walkers out at an open meadow where a stream is crossed. At a junction with a track turn right and head on past the farm of **Montagne du Cros**. Here the path joins a surfaced road which, being a dead end, sees almost no traffic. Pass a *buron* on the left and continue gradually uphill. On meeting the **D27** road and gaining surprising views of the Puy de Dôme, go left for 200m until a drinks/ice cream break-friendly *auberge* and parking area with picnic benches at **Douharesse Haut** are reached.

After Douharesse the track becomes unsurfaced and gives walkers ample opportunity to marvel at the two rock bastions overlooking the valley.

At the end of the **car park** a small surfaced track goes left. Take this towards the hamlet of **Douharesse**. ◄ The track continues for a further 1km until passing a path going right to **le Cros**. Ignore this and keep straight on. Eventually the track swings rightwards and the outbound route returns you to the **parking area**.

WALK 27

A Tour of the Curiosities of St Nectaire

Start/Finish	St Nectaire church above the village off the D150
Distance	9km
Total Ascent	280m
Difficulty	1
Time	3hrs
Highest Point	940m
Map	IGN 1:25,000 Sheet 2432ET *Massif du Sancy*
Public Transport	Twice daily buses from Clermont (July/August only)
Parking	St Nectaire church car park

The attractive village of St Nectaire is widely renowned for its 12th century basilica, along with its thermal spa which dates back to Roman times. The church provides the starting point for a route which explores some of the more esoteric curiosities of the surrounding area. The foremost of these are the troglodyte caves which can be found on the vertiginous slopes of the Puy de Chateauneuf – the high point of the walk. Also of interest *en route* are the various remains of the ancient Auvergne in the form of two dolmens and two menhirs, which provide clues as to the activities of prehistoric man in the area. If you love Time Team, this walk is a must!

Start at the car park for **St Nectaire church** on the steep road above the village. The church is signposted from the main road through the village.

> The **basilica** is named for St Nectarius who was the first evangelist of the region. Religious annals tell of an ancient temple of Apollo on Mont Cornadore, where the church now stands. The church is open daily 9am-7pm and contains a late 12th century Virgin and child statue and many other examples of Auvergne's Romanesque style.

From the church walk down the main road until shortly reaching a cross on a bend, where a small road

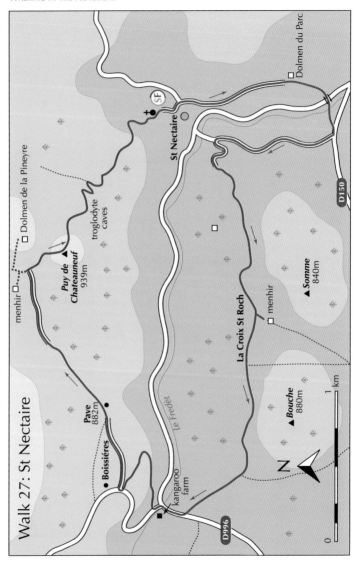

Walk 27: St Nectaire

Dolmen du Parc

D150

Dolmen de la Pineyre

troglodyte caves

Puy de Chateauneuf 939m

menhir

St Nectaire

SF

†

Somme 840m

La Croix St Roch

menhir

Pave 882m

Boissières

Le Fredet

Bouche 880m

kangaroo farm

D996

N

1 km

0

The Dolmen du Parc

leads off left, traversing the hillside to the Dolmen du Parc and tennis court. Take this surfaced minor road for 1km, choosing the lower option at a fork. This brings you to a small park with tennis courts, a folly and the impressive **Dolmen du Parc**, which seems quite incongruous in its landscaped surroundings.

At the dolmen descend beneath the children's play area to follow steps towards the road, with yellow markers. After 70m a pedestrian bridge carries you across the main road. Head through the car park of the casino on the other side, to find another small metal footbridge. Here turn left on a small road and 50m later this will join the bigger **D150**. Turn right for 50m, then take the right hand fork down the minor Chemin de Se, where the lofty St Nectaire church reappears in view. At the brow of a hill after 800m a track comes off left. Take this uphill, joining the GR30, and follow this for 2km. On the first bend ignore a track going left and swing right uphill until levelling out and straightening through pastures.

▶ After 1km at a flat area between the **Somme** and **Bouche** hills a path left uphill to **la Croix St Roch** allows a short deviation of 100m or so to a menhir (standing stone) which sits on a burial mound at the top of a rise. Retrace your steps to the original track and turn left signposted to Bouche.

Views N across the valley to the troglodyte caves occur intermittently.

The track goes through mixed woodland. At a junction of tracks take the right hand way downhill, and after a further 300m this meets the **D996**. Cross the road and turn right on a path beside the road, leading past a **kangaroo farm** which is open to the public. Almost immediately a large parking area is seen where a minor road to **Boissiéres** leads left. Take this and look out for the first track heading right.

Go uphill on this track, which becomes grassy and, after 300m, veers left. Here a track coming off right should be ignored as although it looks like an obvious shortcut on the IGN map, it is mismarked and soon peters out. The track continues uphill until meeting a minor road just before the hamlet of **Bossiéres**.

Take another road right off the bend by an old tower towards **Pavé**. This climbs gradually, and becomes unsurfaced for a while after 300m. After 1.2km reach a sharp left turn where a clear path joins from the right, making a sort of T junction.

Where this surfaced track turns sharply left, our main route takes the clear path going right down the edge of a wheat field.

> Here **two short detours** may be made by enthusiasts. By following your original surfaced track left and uphill for 50m you will see a crossroads of routes with a path going right on a detour to reach the **Dolmen de la Pineyre** in a round trip of 700m. This dolmen has remained untouched as an ancient burial mound with a large stone on top.
>
> Opposite the path to the dolmen there is a track leading in 200m to another **menhir** which is surrounded by peculiar metal boxes covered in fake lawn material – we have no idea why.

From here great views of the church at St Nectaire and the surrounding puys are gained.

Continue on the main route, descending into a forest. A col is eventually passed and a short hike reaches the relatively steep summit of **Puy de Chateauneuf**. Note that the IGN map inaccurately shows the path avoiding this summit. ◄

Saint Nectaire church

Continue over the summit and down log steps. After 50m or so a short path doubles back right and is sign-posted to the grottoes of Chateauneuf. These impressive ancient **troglodyte caves** are worth the short detour and are good fun to explore. From here retrace your steps for 50m back to the original path.

The **castle at Murol**, visible to the SW, sits atop a rocky volcanic abutment and dates from medi-eval times. Every summer a group called Gabriel's Companions dress up in Middle Ages garb and relive the time of the knights in the castle's keep. The castle is open to visitors daily during the summer months.

Head down the hairpins, finding blue markers and ignoring tributary paths. At a bench and a signpost the path widens but views of St Nectaire and the castle at Murol disappear. Continue on the main path, trending leftwards and bringing you into **St Nectaire**. A left turn will take you to the church, where there are two *auberges* and a shop further down the road.

WALK 28
Lake Guéry and the Banne d'Ordanche

Start/Finish	Maison de la Flore ski centre
Distance	12.5 km
Total Ascent	620m
Difficulty	2
Time	4hrs (4hrs 30mins including Puy Loup)
Highest Point	1512m
Map	IGN 1:25,000 Sheet 2432ET *Massif du Sancy*
Parking	Col du Guéry parking area on the D983 to Mont-Dore

This circular walk provides an enjoyable ridge crest outing without the exertion of gaining a colossal amount of height. The lovely glacial Lake Guéry provides a pleasing beginning and end to the excursion and the added benefit of views of the Mortes du Guéry waterfall gives a good distraction en route. The summits of the Banne d'Ordanche (1512m) and Puy Gros (1485m) are worthwhile objectives in themselves, and by combining them a pleasing horseshoe around high pastures can be made, accompanied by lovely views of the Monts Dore, the Puys chain and also the Cantal and Forez mountains.

Follow the path from the **Maison de la Flore** ski centre, marked with yellow markers, until reaching the shore of **Lake Guéry**. Here, skirt the side of the lake rightwards W on intermittent wooden planks. Climb a short slope to meet another path and turn left. After 200m the path bends up right but we take a path going left marked in

Lake Guéry

green which descends to the lake again. After a further 200m, choose the right hand option when the path forks once more. Here the path heads up the right side of the Mortes de Guéry river and leads to an excellent viewing platform for the 15m **cascade** which tumbles over eroded basalt columns.

From the platform continue for 100m then pass through a gate, staying by the river. After 300m cross a stile and turn right on a track for 100m until a junction, where a left turn is taken. The track swings left towards the **1350m spot height**, then continues gradually through closed pasture with good views of the Puy de Sancy. ▶ Around 600m before reaching these cross a cattle grid and a further 200m along brings you to a path which deviates rightwards to the summit of **Puy Loup**.

The Puy May ruins soon become visible ahead.

If this **deviation** is taken then a pleasant ridge crest path can be followed which heads over Puy Loup and the Borne des Quatre Seigneurs col (the meeting point of Mont-Dore's four ancient communes) to the Banne D'Ordanche. Allow 20mins extra for this alternative route.

167

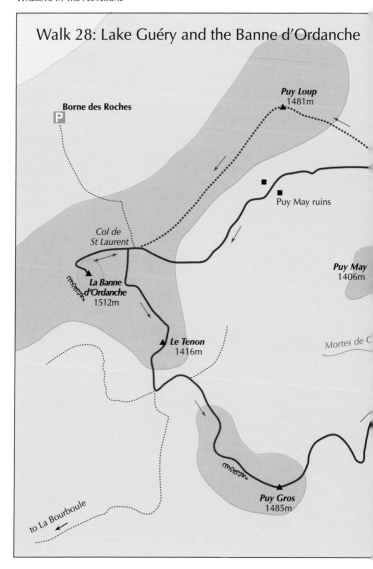

Walk 28: Lake Guéry and the Banne d'Ordanche

Puy Loup
1481m

Borne des Roches

P

Col de
St Laurent

La Banne
d'Ordanche
1512m

Puy May ruins

Puy May
1406m

Le Tenon
1416m

Mortes de C

to La Bourboule

Puy Gros
1485m

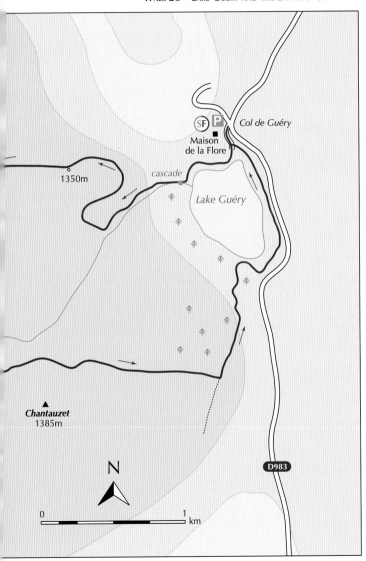

Our main route stays on the lower track past the ruined farm buildings of **Puy May**, around the open hillside and up to the **Col de St Laurent**. Here the track is joined by the ridge crest path. Turn left and go through a metal gate on a grassy path signposted to **Banne d'Ordanche**. This takes a fairly circuitous route round the W side and up to the summit on wooden gangplanks. ◄

Views of the Puys chain, the Sancy massif, Puy Mary and the Monts du Forez are all marked from the **summit orientation table**.

Descend by retracing your steps towards the col, then take a path off right just before reaching the col. This initially descends and can prove slippy in wet weather. Duck under a fence met at the top of a rise, and at a yellow marker turn right, ascending **le Tenon**. The path soon joins a wider track, where a left is taken. After 200m the GR30 is marked right. Take this to ascend the peaty path up the **Puy Gros**, with superb views as you climb to the summit plateau.

From the summit follow red and white markers down an initially steep rocky path, which bends rightwards towards two *burons*. Before these are reached a left turn should be taken at a wooden post. At the corner of a barbed wire fence where a well worn path splits left stay by the fence, following it straight downhill with the fence to your right until a stile allows a crossing near some wooden gangplanks. After crossing the fence pick up a path left which circles **Chantauzet**. Eventually this reaches a wooden stile, from where Lac Guéry is marked. The path becomes enclosed by two fences, climbing initially then descending steeply to the right side of a forest. A forest track is eventually joined. After a further 100m reach a junction with another forest track and turn left to eventually reach the **lake**. At the lake hike around the right hand (E) side using the wide lake shore itself (the W side of the lake proves awkward). At the head of the lake a path leads back to the **Maison de la Flore** and your point of departure.

THE HAUTE-LOIRE
Livradois Forez and Velay

The Lavoûte Polignac château (Walk 30)

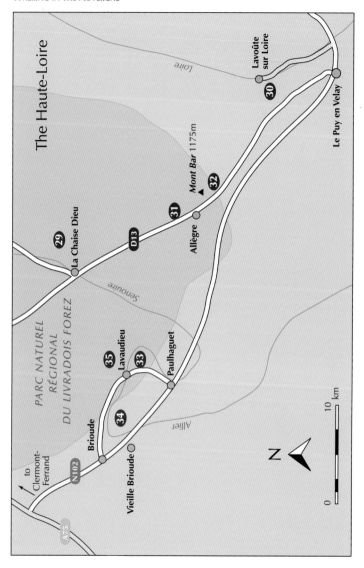

The Haute-Loire

PARC NATUREL RÉGIONAL DU LIVRADOIS FOREZ

to Clermont-Ferrand

N102

A75

Brioude

Vieille Brioude

Lavaudieu

Paulhaguet

La Chaise Dieu

D13

Allègre

Mont Bar 1175m

Le Puy en Velay

Lavoûte sur Loire

Loire

Sénouire

Allier

29
35
33
34
31
32
30

N

0   10 km

INTRODUCTION

This chapter covers the most interesting walking terrain in south-eastern Auvergne. The real appeal of the Haute-Loire is its historic villages, magnificent abbeys and châteaux coupled with pleasant gentle hiking routes through bucolic rural scenery. As well as ancient forests, the *Parc Naturel Régional Livradois-Forez* (Livradois Forez Natural Regional Park) is a protected area of woodlands and traditional farmland characterised by sprawling high plateaus and occasional granite outcrops. The Velay and Craponne areas have plenty of religious and historic features which complement the varied walking terrain. The rivers of the Haute-Loire, including the Senouire, Ceroux and the Loire itself also feature heavily on these itineraries.

The wonderful city base of Le Puy en Velay is famous as a starting point of the Camino de Santiago de Compostela, known in English as The Way of St James. Even for hardened town-avoiders, the city, with its fantasy-like volcanic buttresses and implausibly perched churches and statues, is a must-see destination. Its cathedral is a UNESCO World Heritage Site, but eyes will first be drawn to the cliff-top Chapel of St Michael of Aguilhe, dating from 962,

and the huge iron statue of Notre Dame de France made from 213 Russian cannons seized during the Crimean war.

The Livradois Forez park extends north into the *département* of Puy de Dôme, into Allier and very close to the Montagne Bourbonnaise. The eastern edge of the park forms the Auvergne's border with the Rhône-Alpes region. The densely forested Monts du Forez run along this same border. For walks in this chapter Chaise-Dieu and Allègre are within the Livradois Forez park, Lavaudieu and Domeyrat are at its edge and Vieille Brioude ('Old Brioude') just outside. Allègre is the gateway to the Velay area and Lavôute-sur-Loire is further south still.

Due to the size of the *département*, for convenience this guide features walks in central Haute-Loire which are likely to be easily accessible for those also visiting the Cantal, Monts Dômes or other northern areas. Therefore the Mont Mézenc massif on the Ardèche border more than 25km south of Le Puy is not included on walks in this book, nor are the far-flung Monts du Forez in the east and Monts de la Margeride on the Languedoc border to the southwest.

Walk 29: Around Chaise-Dieu and the Senouire

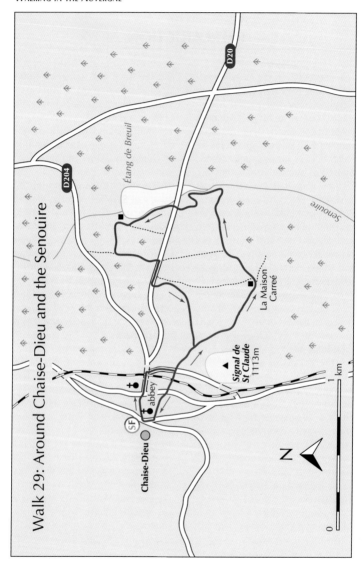

D20

D204

Étang de Breuil

Senouire

La Maison Carreé

Signal de St Claude 1113m

abbey

SF

Chaise-Dieu

N

0   1 km

WALK 29

Around Chaise-Dieu and the Senouire

Start/Finish	La Chaise-Dieu abbey parking area off N102 N of le Puy
Distance	4.5km
Difficulty	1
Time	1hr 30mins
Map	IGN 1:25,000 Sheet 2734O *Allègre/La Chaise Dieu*
Public Transport	2 buses daily from le Puy en Velay. A tourist train from Ambert to Chaise-Dieu runs July-September (www.agrivap.fr)

The square towers of the magnificent abbey of St Robert dominate the village of Chaise-Dieu. The abbey itself, with its superb macabre frescoes, tapestries and gargoyles, is a good enough reason to visit the area, but this short walk makes an attractive outing for those travelling to or from Le Puy en Velay. The hike circles pleasantly through the abbey cloisters across the Chaise-Dieu plateau to the Breuil forest, the river Senouire and Lake Breuil – a good spot for a picnic.

There are numerous *auberges*, hotels, pizzerias and an *office du tourisme* in the village, along with a small supermarket, various art and cheese shops and a cinema. There is also a municipal campsite just out of town. The main abbey building is open to the public from 9am to noon and from 2pm to 6pm June to September with a €4 entry charge.

Parking for the **abbey** is marked from the main road with a green sign. At the bottom right hand corner of the parking area follow a track down to the right of a hotel, seemingly into the abbey. This goes through the spectacular arched cloisters of the Chaise-Dieu and into a lawned quadrangle.

Construction of the **abbey** was started by St Robert in the 11th century and the building had grown to house more than 300 monks by the time of his death. It was 300 years later that the abbey was given some of its more extravagant features when it was taken under the wing of Pope Clement VI who had been a monk there and gave it the name of Chaise-Dieu or 'seat of God'. It then had a turbulent history and the abbey was partially destroyed three times before being restored to its former glory in the 20th century.

Pass through a wooden door and down some steps to the centre of the village, which has a tourist office and a fountain. Turn right, passing beneath the front of the abbey. Now turn right up the north (left) side of the abbey, passing sensational gargoyles. The road leads to the back of the town hall and another parking area where there is a stone archway in the top left hand corner. Go through this, passing a cinema, to come out at a crossroads with the main road. Cross this passing a small chapel on the left and follow the **D20** towards Malvieres. After 100m pass beneath a **railway line** through a narrow arch. Turn right immediately after this and after 60m take a signed route towards **Signal de St Claude**.

After 100m turn left on a path signed Le Serpent d'Or. Leave the surfaced road here and join a track. This forks after 60m and the right hand way is taken. There is a sign about the Serpent route marked left but stay right on a sandy track. You will reach a small ruin called **La Maison Carrée**. ◄

This used to be a storage place for the abbatial monks but was later used as a smugglers' den.

Take a left fork off the rubbly track heading into the forest of Breuil, where legend has it that the lumpy trees are a result of spirits curing a hunchback of his hump and transferring his infirmity to the nearby trees.

After 100m in the forest a clearing is reached. Here take a faint grassy track veering left which passes a small easily missed carved stone (this is the Serpent d'Or carving).

Now find a clear forest track heading left. Ignore a first track off to the right after 200m and continue for a further 200m to where a red number ten is painted on a tree, next to which a small information post can be seen. Take this well-walked path descending through forest over a small wooden bridge which crosses a stream. Soon cross a forest road and head straight on along the wide grassy path down to the **Senouire river** – at this point no more than a brook – and veer left along the mossy course of the winding water, which seems barely to move.

> The signs pointing to the mysterious **Serpent d'Or** or 'golden snake' actually mean the river Senouire, which is small and sinuous here. The name of the river is a shortened form of Serpent d'Or and is so-called due to the snaking way it winds through the forest, and the presence of iron in the water, giving it a golden glow.

At a small concrete bar in the river stay on the main path which veers left then bends back right and crosses a series of small bridges. The path brings you out at the **Étang de Breuil** lake.

Follow the path round the left (W) bank of the lake to the northern end, where there is a small dam and electric works. Here take a forest track going left for 200m until a crossroads of tracks is encountered. At the crossroads go straight across onto a grassy track. This veers left and a further 300m brings you to the **D20** road, which you

Beside the Étang de Breuil

The abbey at Chaise-Dieu

follow right for 60m until a path left is taken which eventually leaves the forest to ascend through pasture. When the track joins tarmac turn right and then take a left at a fire station. Here go through a square bridge tunnel under the **railway**. Cross the road to return to the village and **abbey**.

WALK 30
The Gorges of the Loire

Start/Finish	Lavoûte-sur-Loire, 11km N of le Puy
Distance	11km
Total Ascent	320m
Difficulty	2
Time	3hrs 40mins
Highest Point	860m
Map	IGN 1:25,000 Sheet 2735E *Le Puy en Velay*
Public Transport	3 trains/day from le Puy to Lavoûte but not convenient times. Buses every 2hrs from le Puy to Lavoûte
Parking	In village on S side of the river by bridge

The river Loire is famous for its many beautiful chateaux and this stretch in the Auvergne's Haute-Loire department is no exception. The route takes hikers past the 15th century Chateau de Lavoûte-Polignac on the return leg of the trip.

The river Loire here is still not at its most potent. It rises on the slopes of Mont Gerbier de Jonc in the Ardèche about 100km SE and has 900km of its journey to the sea yet to run. Despite its infancy, the power of the river has been visibly harnessed in this area with two hydroelectric dams on route. Views from the ridge above the Loire gorge also stretch to the summits of the Menzenc massif on the border of the Ardèche region.

Start in the village on the S side of the river by the main road bridge. Here there is a **parking area**, a church and some public toilets. From the car park head N, crossing the **Loire** by the road bridge, and take the first left up a small road signed to Tholance and a viewpoint. Follow this for 300m, going under the **railway line**, where an immediate left is taken. Follow this small surfaced road by the side of the river for nearly 1km as the Loire makes its way into a gorge. You will pass the new railway bridge and subsequently an old ruined **Roman bridge** with its fragile arches over the Loire.

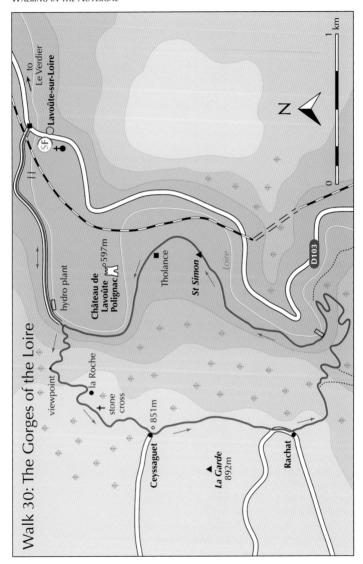

Walk 30: The Gorges of the Loire

to Le Verdier

Lavoûte-sur-Loire

SF

hydro plant

Château de Lavoûte Polignac 597m

Tholance

St Simon

Loire

D103

viewpoint

la Roche

stone cross

851m

Ceyssaguet

La Garde 892m

Rachat

N

1 km

0

After 1km a path can be seen heading uphill right marked with red and yellow. Ignore a previous path marked with a red and white cross. The path heads steeply up into the forest and up the side of the Loire gorge. The route is also one of the linked paths of the Camino of St James and is marked with a flashing light symbol on a blue background. The rocky path climbs via switchbacks providing occasional glimpses of the Loire bridges. Continue on the main path to reach the tiny hamlet of **la Roche**. Go up steeply through the hamlet, following now red and white waymarkers and veering left at the highest point of the hamlet. The path soon narrows on leaving la Roche. A **stone cross** passed to the left offers a good overlook of the castle and Loire bridges.

The path delivers you simply enough to another hamlet, **Ceyssaguet**, where a surfaced track will join from the right. Go left on the unsurfaced track here. After 50m ignore a path branching left and continue on the sandy track. Follow red waymarkers towards **Rachat**. The track reaches a surfaced road where you turn left into the hamlet and a communal bread oven is passed to your right. Go straight on along a track. This bends left and 100m later take a left fork marked in red going downhill. ▸

Here the descent to the Loire begins.

Take care as the navigation can prove confusing here. Look out for a sign marking the GR3 to Chanceau and take the left hand track following yellow waymarkers. After 80m this track swings back right. Ignore a first track coming off left on the hairpin and follow the red gravel track down by the side of fields. At a sharp right turn in the red track at the corner of a field there is a pine tree. Do not follow the track here but come off left on an easily missed path which is originally marked with a yellow cross but soon yellow waymarkers appear. This is a **path**, *not* a track. If you find yourself descending into the forest on a track turn back and look for the path, otherwise you willl add much distance to your hike. The path heads downhill through the forest until eventually descending all the way to the river where a left turn is taken.

The path now follows the **river Loire** back to our starting point. It becomes narrow and overgrown in parts

Looking down on Lavoûte sur Loire

working its way towards a dam in the river. On reaching the dam the path climbs steeply to negotiate cliffs then levels out on the hillside above the river. Approaching **St Simon** pass through a gate and descend on a less distinct path to **Tholance** and cross a fence, turning left onto a track which soon becomes a surfaced road. Passing through the hamlet the **Chateau de Lavoûte-Polignac** can be marvelled at. ▸

Follow the small road back to join the outbound route near the first dam and mill.

The **château at Lavoûte** has been in the hands of Velay nobles the Polignac family since it was built. It was seized as a national asset during the revolution but was quickly bought back by the family once aristocratic property ownership became acceptable again.

WALK 31
A Circuit of Allègre

Start/Finish	Allègre
Distance	6km
Total Ascent	140m
Difficulty	1
Time	1hr 30mins
Highest Point	1080m
Map	IGN 1:25,000 Sheet 2734O *Allègre/La Chaise Dieu*
Parking	In village centre

Rising on the slopes of Mont Baury, the village of Allègre makes a wonderful base from which to explore the lower part of the Livradois Forez park and the attractive Portes de Auvergne area stretching down to le Puy en Velay. Allègre is dominated by the vestiges of a 14th century castle, with its double towers standing like sentries over the surrounding landscape. Allègre has several hotels and restaurants. There is a pleasant municipal campsite open mid June-September and a tourist information office also open in peak season which contains a small museum of vulcanology.

This short walk provides excellent views of the castle – known as the Potence – and the gentle countryside surrounding it, which is both pastoral and volcanic.

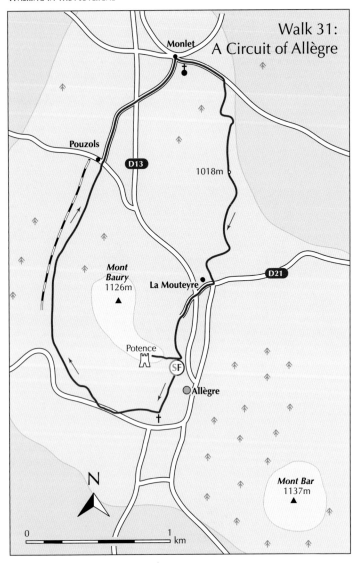

Walk 31:
A Circuit of Allègre

Monlet

Pouzols

D13

1018m

Mont
Baury
1126m

La Mouteyre

D21

Potence

SF

Allègre

N

Mont Bar
1137m

0   1
                     km

Start in the village centre. Facing uphill towards the elegant Porte de Monsieur doorway, ascend steps on its left following red and yellow waymarkers leading initially up towards the Potence. Where a yellow marked route goes off left continue straight up to reach the **Potence** and a viewing platform.

The Porte de Monsieur at Allègre

> The Potence at Allègre was **part of a huge castle** comprising 11 towers all linked by an ornate lofty walkway. At the centre was a dungeon. The majority of the castle was destroyed by fire in 1698. The two linked towers of the Potence, along with the imposing outer gates of Porte de Monsieur and Porte de Ravel are now all that remain.

Allow five minutes to reach this and five minutes to get back to the original route.

On rejoining this take the yellow marked path to the right of a wall. This soon joins a track and passes an ancient **stone cross**. Head straight on, ignoring another track which branches off right. After 700m a bridge over a disused **railway line** is seen on the left.

185

The Potence

The **rail line** linked the villages of Darsac and Craponne. It was opened in 1902 and served to transport local wood further afield.

Do not cross the bridge but continue on the track which runs beside the line for a further 800m until reaching the hamlet of **Pouzols**.

At Pouzols the track meets a surfaced road. Head straight along this, remaining parallel to the railway line at first. Cross the **D13** and continue into the pretty village of **Monlet**.

At the village's 13th century Romanesque **church**, which was used by the monks of Chaise-Dieu in the 15th century, you will find a golden crucifix and a water fountain beside a painted soldier war memorial.

Beneath the church a road descends signposted to Chardon. Take this, going between the crucifix and the war memorial and continue for 200m until a track comes off to your right at a cross commemorating the life of Caroline Tournier. ▶ After 100m the track starts to climb up to a plateau and the **1018m spot height**. Here the forest track ends, but head straight on taking a path which follows the right hand edge of a wheat field and the left edge of the forest. Ahead the forested volcanic dome of **Mont Bar** is visible and, as the forest dissipates, the Potence of Allègre rears up. At the end of the wheat field the path becomes a little indistinct but head straight on and after 70m a yellow waymarker can be spotted on a post and the ancient route works its way pleasantly between the fields. Follow the path between fences, eventually bringing you out at a track. Go left here towards **la Mouteyre**. On reaching the **D21** road turn right and continue to access the upper part of Allègre.

The track is rough and earthen but faint yellow waymarkers can still be spotted heading downhill into the forest.

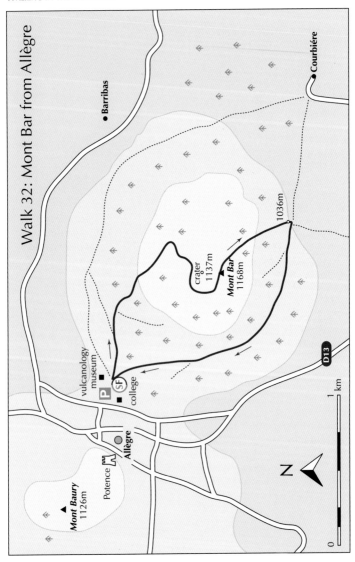

Walk 32: Mont Bar from Allègre

WALK 32

Mont Bar from Allègre

Start/Finish	Allègre
Distance	4km
Total Ascent	200m
Difficulty	1
Time	1hr 15mins
Highest Point	1150m
Map	IGN 1:25,000 Sheet 2734O *Allègre/La Chaise Dieu*
Parking	At college E of village centre

This short walk is a good twin to the first Allègre route (Walk 31). It ascends the unique Mont Bar volcano – its singularity is born of the fact that it is the only strombolian peak to have an ancient marsh ecosystem called a *tourbière* in its summit crater. Mont Bar was formed from pressure inside faults in the granite plateau underneath the Massif Central. The volcano's last explosion was 800,000 years ago but the *tourbière* was formed by a lake that has been gone for a mere 8,000 years. Along the path to the crater's rim good examples of volcanic 'bombes' or lumps of fused lava rock can be seen underfoot. The route remains shaded and is a good option for a boiling hot afternoon. For further information about the formation of a *tourbière*, see Walk 41.

Park in the **designated area** by the college, E of and downhill from the village centre. Leave the parking area on an obvious path heading steeply uphill. The path is wide and uneven. Amble up through the forest to easily reach the rim of **Mont Bar's crater**. Head straight over the rim following red and white waymarkers down into the crater.

Legend has it that **Mont Bar** was formed by a huge underground furnace where the Cyclops was working away for months to make a throne for Zeus. The grassy marsh of the *tourbière* is seen to your left

Allègre through the trees

and numerous nature trail boards explain the fragile ecosystem of the area.

In the early 19th century, local peasants decided that it would be a good idea to build a drain from the Mont Bar crater in order to dry out the deforested part of the mountain and create a pasture for their animals. In attempting this work, one lucky worker found a massive hoard of Roman coins and jewellery in the tourbière. However, the drainage plan was soon declared unsuccessful.

Having traversed the crater, the red marked track heads steeply down on bouldery terrain. After 600m descend to a sign marking an altitude of **1036m**. Take care to turn right on a path here marked as 'Tour de Volcans' and 'Allègre'. The path contours around the hillside through mixed pines. Pass two more small clearings until emerging to eventual superb views of Allègre and its impressive Potence ruins perched at the top of the village. The path leads back to the **college** and tourist information centre.

WALK 33

Domeyrat and the Senouire

Start/Finish	Domeyrat
Distance	5.5km
Difficulty	1
Time	1hr 40mins
Map	IGN 1:25,000 Sheet 2634E *Paulhaguet*
Parking	By the old bridge in the centre of the village

The village of Domeyrat, with its ruined 13th century castle and pretty footbridge over the Senouire, makes a pleasant starting point for this route. The castle's noticeboards are proud to boast of its superb location on a rocky promontory at a bend in the river overlooking the surrounding area – this seems fair as during its 700 years no 'bloody battle or murderous siege' has ever troubled sleepy Domeyrat. The described walk takes hikers off the beaten track into the heart of the Haute-Loire region.

From the **old bridge** in the centre of the village cross the new road bridge heading S and pace up the road, passing

Looking down on the Senouire from the bridge at Domeyrat

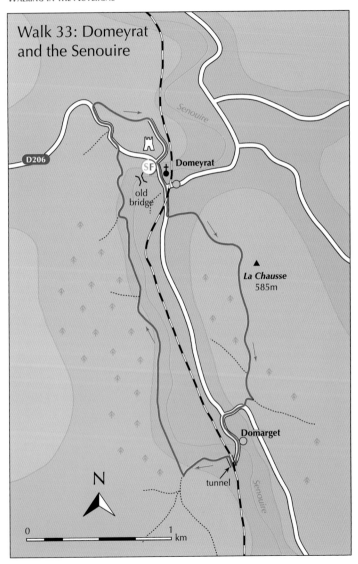

Walk 33: Domeyrat
and the Senouire

D206

Domeyrat

old
bridge

SF

Senouire

La Chausse
585m

Domarget

tunnel

Senouire

N

0   1
                    km

the impressive Saint Roch **church**. After 100m reach the town hall on your right and cross a railway bridge. Here turn right along a surfaced road marked with walking signs. After 80m our route branches left just after a wrought iron **cross** marked with yellow waymarkers on a wide grassy path.

> Domeyrat's 13th century **castle** has a chequered history of plague, desertion and partial ruin during the revolutionary years. In two of its tubular towers 16th century paintings still survive showing hunting and religious scenes.

Continue to head up the hill. Here the path narrows and could be muddy after rain. ▶ At the top of the hill emerge into the open pasture of **La Chausse** – this area was used as a depot for arms during World War II by the French Resistance. Routefinding care must be taken here. Strike across the field in the direction of a yellow marker, looking for a similar one in the opposite corner. The route becomes easier to follow after this. Having crossed 150m of open pasture follow a farm track through a gap in a fence and continue down left to more markers. Eventually a minor road is met. Take this right, ignoring yellow waymarkers, and enter the village of **Domarget**. A strange lone pine in a grassy circle is its centrepiece.

Take a left fork off the main road where it bends to the right. In 50m you will pass a railway bridge to your right but do not cross this. Head on another 100m to a bridge across the **Senouire river**. Having crossed this, continue on the minor road for 50m then take a path going right through a square tunnel under the **railway line**. ▶ After the tunnel turn left up an overgrown path which runs parallel to the railway for 60m then bends right and ascends pleasantly above the old mill. The path levels off and traces the course of the Senouire on its left side for the most part, temporarily leaving the river to follow the edge of a wheat field and meet a bigger path where a sharp right turn is taken to return towards the river embankment.

In season wild strawberries grow and await picking.

To the right is an old mill wheel.

The path widens to join a farm track at open ground. When the **D206** road on the outskirts of **Domeyrat** is met, those wanting a closer look at the castle will turn left for 400m to a picnic area. Here go right up to the château on a well worn track. A road on the castle's E side leads back to the river.

WALK 34

Vieille Brioude and the Ceroux

Start/Finish	Place de la Croix de Pres, Vieille Brioude
Distance	11km
Total Ascent	300m
Difficulty	2
Time	3hrs 15mins
Highest Point	730m
Map	IGN 1:25,000 Sheet 2634O *Brioude*
Public Transport	Train to Brioude from le Puy or bus to Old Brioude from le Puy
Parking	Parking area just off the main road at Place de la Croix de Pres

This enjoyable excursion has been included primarily for its situation on the main route between the hubs of Clermont-Ferrand and le Puy en Velay. Any visitor to the Auvergne's primary walking regions is likely to pass close to Brioude on the N102 or A75 roads, and this hike provides a good excuse to stop *en route* north or south. Vieille Brioude ('Old Brioude') has some charming churches and a castle. The walk takes hikers to the Ceroux river cascades and gains height to view the Allier gorge. There are also vestiges of ancient Auvergne on route: several burial mounds and standing stones lay nearby, although these can be difficult to spot.

There are plenty of shops, hotels and bars in Brioude. Near the starting point of the walk there is also an open-air wine-making exhibit.

Start at the Place de la Croix de Pres. From the **parking area** cross the main road and take the **Rue des Vignes** down the left side of the Hotel des Glycines. After 150m the road is followed left and after a further 70m turn left again onto a very small road which brings you to a junction with the **D585** at the entry to **Vieille Brioude**. Turn right here for a short section on this busy road. Cross the road bridge and take a right immediately after up a rough track.

The track climbs through the woods and is followed for more than 1km until a crossroads of paths. Take the right hand path downhill. This path soon widens. Ignore a path coming off left above **la Pruneyre**. On arriving at

Vieille Brioude perched above the Ceroux

195

Walk 34: Vieille Brioude and the Ceroux

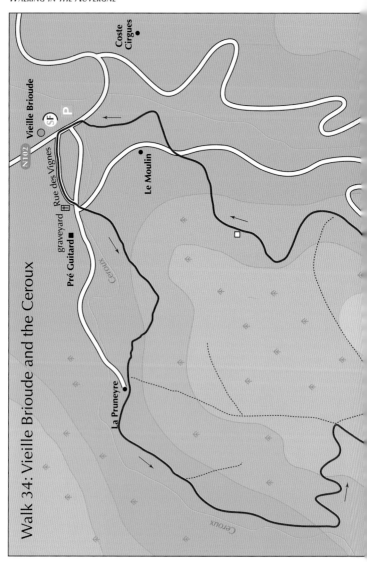

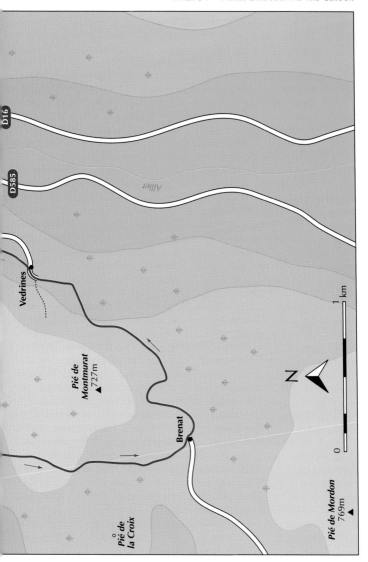

D16

D585

Allier

Vedrines

Pié de
Montmurat
▲ 727m

Brenat

Pié de
la Croix

Pié de Mordon
769m ▲

N

1 km

0

197

Here there is a
warning sign for
falling rocks and
subsidence.

the picturesque hamlet, the track joins a surfaced lane
and turns left continuing for a further 50m until becoming a path once more on a steep banking above the
river. ◄ The narrow path wanders above a steep drop
to the **River Ceroux**. Eventually this draws level with the
river at a small waterfall. Follow the river until a crossroads of paths by a small island in the river. Turn left up a
wide path and follow yellow markers uphill through the
oak and pine woods to a junction. Do not turn right here
but go left for 30m until four tracks meet and then take a
right turn with a yellow marker.

The track gains a high ridge and panoramic views left
to the Allier valley and Livradois Forez and right to Mont
Mouchet appear. Eventually the forest is left behind and
farmed land is crossed to meet a larger track where you
turn left. Stay on this as it contours the **Pie de la Croix** hill
and winds down into the pretty hamlet of **Brenat**. Follow
yellow markers and a surfaced road to the village 'trian-
gle'. Here take a track going left, passing an orchard on
your right and commence the descent to Védrines on an
easy sandy track.

At the slightly eerie village of **Védrines** meet a surfaced road going past a dry fountain. After 50m and
opposite a large barn take a sandy track left. Follow this,
eventually climbing to a small pass between the hills. At
this col on the left you will see an ancient standing stone.
From here descend on the main track down to **le Moulin**.
The final section of this is surfaced. At a junction with
the **D585** turn left for 40m then take a path on your right
at a white cross with views of the 12th century church
of St Vincent at Vieille Brioude. Follow the path down to
the **River Ceroux**. After crossing the bridge ignore the first
right and take the second right uphill along the Rue de
Pavat to get to **Vieille Brioude**. Head through the tunnel
at a small square and go up some stone steps. Here a left
will take you to the **church** and right will take you back
to the **parking area**.

WALK 35

Lavaudieu Abbey and the Senouire

Start/Finish	Lavaudieu village between Paulhaguet and Brioude on the N102 Le Puy to Clermont road
Distance	10km
Total Ascent	120m
Difficulty	1
Time	2hrs 45min
Highest Point	547m
Map	IGN 1:25,000 Sheet 2634E *Paulhaguet*
Parking	Car park on N side of the river near to the village by road bridge

Lavaudieu is an odd place. It is designated by the French tourist board as one of the most beautiful villages in France. The tourists that this status brings has meant that visitors' cars are banned from the village and parking is widely signposted on the outskirts. The main claim to fame of the village is the waterside St Andre Benedictine abbey. Lavaudieu gets its name from la vallée de Dieu or 'the valley of God'. The village, with its cloisters and winegrowers' cottages, is exceptionally picturesque and the Senouire valley provides a worthwhile hike to accompany a visit.

Lavaudieu has a tourist information office which arranges tours of the abbey and its religious art museum, along with bars, restaurants and *auberges*.

From the **car park** follow the **Senouire river** downstream on the N bank along a wide concrete path beneath the main tower of the abbey **church** itself. Pass by a second extremely narrow road bridge and after a short rise continue on the road in the same direction downhill then heading left back to the river. Here the surfaced road finishes and becomes a track.

After 50m this becomes a riverside path. A rock buttress is passed on the right after 200m. Here the valley narrows substantially. The path trends right uphill leaving the course of the river crossing a pasture where a disused

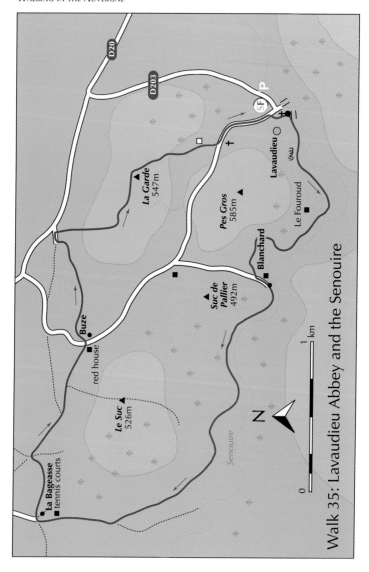

Walk 35: Lavaudieu Abbey and the Senouire

Beneath the abbey of Lavaudieu

building can be seen up right marked as **le Fouroud**. An old path marked on the IGN maps once came off left here but this is no longer navigable so stay straight ahead to gain further height above the river, with woods on the left and pasture on the right. The path now levels out and continues pleasantly. After 1km the path goes left at pastures and then continues to the hamlet of Blanchard. Another smattering of dwellings are seen further uphill to the right on the slopes of **Suc de Palier**. Pass a small electric works before joining a surfaced road. Turn left here to descend and reach the two dwellings at **Blanchard**.

Here there is a ford across the river and the road becomes a track again. ▶ The route continues at river level in the woods on the N side. After passing an unlikely clearing the path forks and you take the right option steeply up through the woods, with a small sign for walkers. Just as all hope of ever leaving the forest is expunged you emerge from the woods and continue along the side of a wheat field, providing much needed relief from the canopy. Another track joins here from the left. Just as the first buildings of **la Bageasse** are seen the track forks and the left hand option is taken, keeping the

This area seems to be popular with fishermen and wild campers.

tennis courts to your right. The track now joins a surfaced road but after 15m take a grassy track to the right with a yellow waymarker.

In 400m the track bends left and meets a more used track. Here turn left for 40m and then right on another track. Ignore branches to the left and right, eventually passing a **red house** on your right and joining a surfaced lane leading to the small settlement of **Buze** and a cross-roads of tracks. Here look for the first track descending right due E. After 400m ignore a right hand fork and continue left (a track marked straight ahead on the IGN map does not exist) to another junction where you will go right for 40m and reach a main road. Without walking along the main road take a track immediately back right S going uphill where keeping left leads over the summit of **la Garde** (547m). Continue on the track, passing a couple of **farm buildings**, eventually joining a surfaced road which leads downhill to the Lavaudieu abbey.

THE MONTAGNE BOURBONNAISE

Clambering up beside the upper falls of the Pisserote (Walk 40)

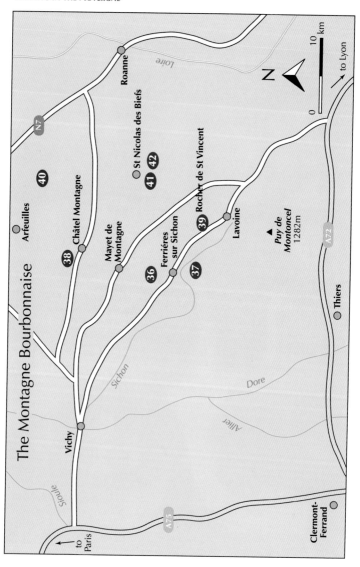

The Montagne Bourbonnaise

INTRODUCTION

Close to the spa town of Vichy – famous for mints and being the centre of occupied France – is the little-known yet nonetheless appealing Montagne Bourbonnaise area (also called the Monts de la Madeleine). With rolling hills, tranquil countryside and numerous attractive rustic villages, the area proves a perfect antidote to the hectic demands of 21st-century living. Should the tempo of life move any slower here it would be stationary: an island of absolute peace in which to unwind among the friendly and occasionally quirky inhabitants, this is an area of great beauty where villagers still enjoy ancient traditions and where pastimes have little changed in 400 years. Tourism has remained at a relatively low level despite numerous information offices, plentiful high quality restaurants and good facilities such as local small-scale ski resorts and even a phenomenal high-wire forest adventure course.

This is the premier walking area of the Allier department, and therefore the Northern Auvergne, and the routes described here tend to be gentle affairs, the perfect length to work up a good appetite for the rustic cuisine of the numerous *auberges* – which even your Yorkshire-born authors feel are good value for money! Decorated with many chateaux from the 12th–18th centuries, picturesque churches, occasional volcanic features such as the Rocher St Vincent, ancient mills and waterfalls, and a superb summer climate where the air tends to fill with butterflies and always feels fresh, the Montagne Bourbonnaise offers a great place to nip off the beaten track and rejuvenate.

There are several good choices of base in the area. The stately city of Vichy is worth visiting but is not truly in the Montagne Bourbonnaise and is not recommended as a walking base due to its size. Far better to immerse oneself in the rural charm of the area and stay in one of the *chambres d'hôtes* or *gîtes* in the villages or hamlets of the Bourbonnaise. The pretty village of Mayet de Montagne is a good option and amenities include two campsites, several hotels, restaurants and many *gîtes*, along with a supermarket, shops and tourist office. Nearby Ferriéres sur Sichon is smaller but also attractive and has one *auberge*, one restaurant, a bakery, a shop, a campsite and *gîtes*. Both Ferriéres and Mayet can be reached by public transport. Further north St Nicolas des Biefs is tucked away in the heart of the mountains and is smaller still, with fewer facilities. The picturesque hilltop village of Châtel Montagne also offers a range of accommodation, including a campsite.

WALK 36
The Ruins of Montgilbert

Start/Finish	Ferriéres sur Sichon War Memorial
Distance	10km
Total Ascent	350m
Difficulty	2
Time	3–3½hrs
Highest Point	660m
Map	IGN 1:25,000 Sheet 2730O *Le Mayet-de-Montagne*
Public Transport	Bus to Ferriéres from Vichy
Parking	At village war memorial, by church or by the *auberge*

Ferriéres sur Sichon is a traditional slow-paced Montagne Bourbonnaise village which boasts a splendid church, a superb auberge, campsite with a fishing lake and an excellent bakery. This wonderful walk climbs above the village to wind its way to the atmospheric ruined 13th-century castle at Montgilbert, passing through sleepy hamlets and along pleasant flower-filled lanes on route.

From the **war memorial** cross the bridge by a pretty village washstand that was used by residents to do laundry until the advent of piped water to the village in the 1960s. Take the road left, passing to the right of the Ferriéres château. After only 100m cross the **D995** and take the rightwards trending track opposite uphill and follow it as it works its way to the sleepy collection of farm buildings which make up **Les Olliéres**.

Here the GR de Pays Montagne Bourbonnaise route is intersected. This is marked with red and white way-markers. Follow these left (W) on an excellent lofty track along the crest of the hill for 1.3km. The path is joined by another track at a **cross** above the farm of **Boudet**. Continue downhill for 200m then take the first right following this for a further 150m until meeting a surfaced road. Here turn right and continue for 1km through **Recost** to the Château Montgilbert parking area. Find the

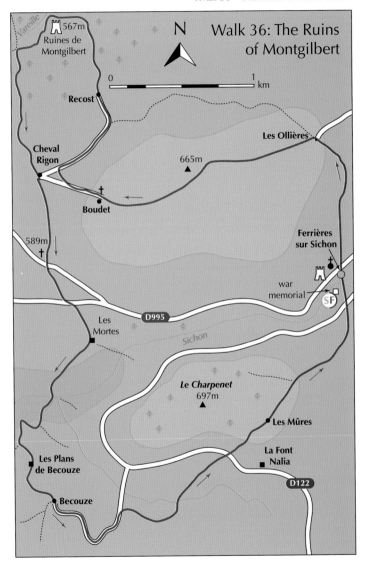

Walk 36: The Ruins of Montgilbert

The 13th century ruins of Montgilbert

stone arch of the main gateway of **Montgilbert**, which is always open and free to wander around.

Montgilbert castle was built in 1250, although parts have since been added. It was owned by various noblemen and Bourbonnaise gentry for the next 500 years until Jean Duprat and his mother moved in during the 1770s. Distraught to find that her new home was such an unfashionable residence, Jean's mother ordered the castle's roof to be removed in order to force her son to leave their home. Since then the castle has been in disrepair and during the 19th century locals used it as a stone quarry to improve their own homes. In 1973 the castle was protected and restoration work began.

Follow the path up to the highest point of the castle grounds. In the NE corner there is another stone doorway. Exit Montgilbert by this and see three paths which head left (W). Take the middle option, which descends a man-made platform below the castle. From here the path dips W into the woods. After 100m there is a fork. Take the right option which is overgrown at first but eventually well walked. Soon the **Vareille river** can be heard below to the right and the path is joined by another ascending from the waterside. After 400m the path joins a wide track which crosses a stream and leads to a grassy cross-roads. Turn leftwards up the grassy track towards **Cheval Rigon**. The track continues steadily enough to **Cheval Rigon** with its proud chestnut tree. Turn left at the first crossroads. After another 100m meet another crossroads and here head straight across.

The track from Cheval Rigon is followed for 300m to a metal **cross** at 589m. Once again cross the **D995** and go down the track directly opposite. After 400m another small road is crossed and a surfaced track leads to **Les Mortes**. These farm buildings should be passed on your left. Continue to follow the track descending into the forest where the **river Sichon** is crossed by way of a wooden bridge.

They don't make them like they used to: old tractor in the Montagne Bourbonnaise

Having crossed the river, ignore a track going leftwards and continue on the main track, climbing over a nose of land for 150m before descending and crossing a tributary stream via another small bridge. Here the wide track leads steeply uphill for 400m until a sharp left turn can be taken. This leads to **les Plans de Becouze** and eventually **Becouze**. At Becouze take the road downhill (left) which signposts Ferriéres steeply for 500m until a clear marked track can be taken rightwards into the forest. Stay on the main path here which eventually crosses the tributary at a bridge and ford. ◀ The track soon climbs out of the forest until reaching the **D122** main road. Cross this and take a lane directly opposite uphill for 250m, passing the hamlet of **Les Mûres** to your right, and where a small **cross** is seen to the left. After a further 350m the road begins to bend round to the right. Here take a track heading straight on. Follow this until meeting a T junction with another track where a left turn sets you on a good winding route to **Ferriéres**. On entering the village you will pass a tractor garage opposite the **war memorial**, where you are virtually guaranteed to see the owner's dogs milling about on the roof of the building barking at strangers.

Here the IGN map marks a lake which categorically does not exist.

WALK 37
Milling around the Mills

Start/Finish	Ferriéres sur Sichon War Memorial
Distance	10km
Total Ascent	360m
Difficulty	1
Time	3hrs
Highest Point	767m
Map	IGN 1:25,000 Sheet 2730O *Mayet de Montagne*
Public Transport	Trans Allier buses to Ferriéres from Vichy
Parking	At village war memorial, by church or by the *auberge*

This is a decent ramble through quiet hamlets and rolling hills tamed by ancient farmers. It links the 'moulins' or mills on the Sichon at Ferriéres and Moulin Neuf. The height gained affords wonderful views of an attractive part of the Montagne Bourbonnaise including a castle, crags and decorative crosses along the way. Also visible on route is a remaining viaduct of the Ferrieres-Lavoine extension to the Cusset-Ferrieres railway line, which opened in 1910, but closed in 1950.

Start at the war memorial at the bottom of the village, where there are public toilets and a nearby drinking fountain.

Never forgotten: the war memorial at Ferriéres sur Sichon

211

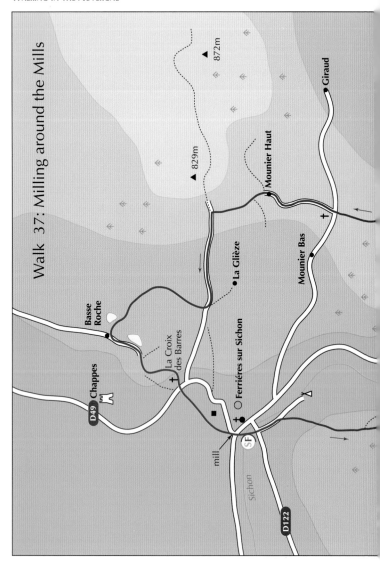

Walk 37: Milling around the Mills

872m

829m

Giraud

Mounier Haut

Mounier Bas

La Glièze

Basse Roche

La Croix des Barres

Chappes

D49

Ferrières sur Sichon

mill

SF

Sichon

D122

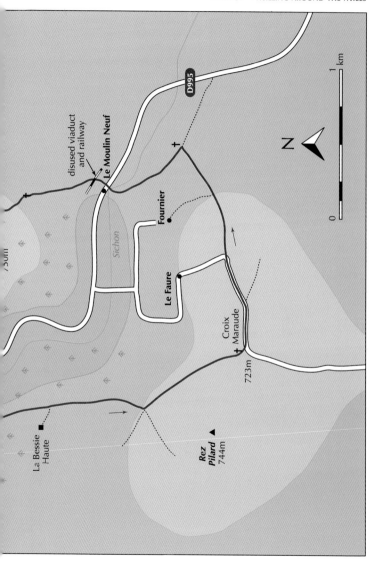

disused viaduct
and railway

Le Moulin Neuf

D995

Sichon

Fournier

Le Faure

Croix
Maraude
723m

La Bessie
Haute

Rez
Pilard
744m

N

0   1 km

Take a minute to discover the first **mill** of the walk, which is situated behind the bakery across the river from the parking area. The old wheel and mill chase is quaintly attractive. On the same side of the river-bank is the pretty old village **washstand**, which is usually blooming with hanging baskets nowadays. This was used by local women for doing laundry until the 1960s when the village homes got a mains water supply.

From here take the road opposite, signposted to a **campsite**. After 100m the surfaced road goes left to the campsite but fork right, heading straight uphill on a rough track.

- **Wild boar** (called *le sanglier*) are prevalent in the Montagne Bourbonnaise. These unpredictable crea-tures, which populate the forests and can roam for hundreds of kilometres, are particularly popular with local hunters.

Passing the floral hamlet of Moulin Neuf

Staying with the main track leads to a triangular junction. Continue uphill on the left route here to reach a crossroads at the **723m spot height**. Turn left on a

surfaced road and after 100m take a left fork marked to Ferriéres. Descend for 400m until a sharp bend in the road. Here continue straight ahead, leaving the road on a track. ▶ The track now continues, making a sharp left at a small iron **cross**, and leads to the hamlet of **Le Moulin Neuf**, where the old railway bridge above it will be seen. Cross the **Sichon** by way of a bridge. You are now upstream of Ferriéres.

Here are clear views of the Rocher St Vincent to the SE and the controversial 2010 windfarm on the La Ligue ridge.

On reaching Le Moulin Neuf an old stone mill wheel remains by the former mill and the track goes uphill to meet the road. Head up a path to the left of the **viaduct**. ▶ The track passes beneath the viaduct and climbs steeply for 1km, passing a **cross** after 500m. Eventually reach a junction with a surfaced road. Take this straight uphill towards **Mounier Haut** – the hamlet that time forgot. At the hamlet continue straight ahead. The road becomes unsurfaced at a picnic bench. After 300m meet the GR de Pays Montagne Bourbonnaise. This is taken left for 600m downhill on a surfaced road. ▶ Take a right turn on a track which skirts the side of a forest. In 200m fork left, descending to gain a view of the privately owned château of **Chappes** and neighbouring hamlets.

This was on the Cusset–Lavoine line constructed in 1910.

Gaps in the trees permit a vista across the pastoral rolling hills of the northern Montagne Bourbonnaise.

The **château** was built in 1470 under the instruction of the Duke of Bourbon. The castle was thought to be ideally situated in a valley surrounded by streams and steep banks. It was constructed in a diamond shape with round towers at the corners and a drawbridge at the main entrance.

The track descends to a tiny fishing lake at **Basse Roche**, where there is also a cross. Here join a surfaced road and turn left for 300m, passing another **pond** and a track forking left which should be ignored until a further 100m brings you to a second clear track which now should be taken left. This immediately crosses a stream and ascends through woods and mounts a hill. Descend again to meet a surfaced road above **Ferriéres**. At the main road take a right for 30m followed by an immediate left on a track leading to the village centre via the back of the school.

WALK 38

Around Châtel Montagne and the Puy de Roc

Start/Finish	Châtel Montagne church
Distance	9km
Difficulty	1
Time	2hrs 45mins
Map	IGN 1:25,000 Sheet 2729O *Lapalisse*
Public Transport	Limited Trans Allier service from Vichy to Châtel
Parking	Large car park in front of the church

This route provides a gentle pastoral ramble around the beautiful high environs of the Montagne Bourbonnaise from the lovely village of Châtel Montagne, with its magnificent 12th century church and incorporates the quirky summit of Puy de Roc. The hike passes through undulating landscapes that evoke a peaceful ancient way of life and visits several well preserved old farming hamlets. There is no major height gain yet the walk affords tremendous elevated views of both the village and the distant principal summits of the Monts Dômes and Dore, particularly from the look-out at Puy de Roc, which is approached via a curious line of crucifixes.

Châtel Montagne itself has a campsite, hotel and restaurants along with a bakery and various shops selling art, trinkets and regional produce.

Facing the **church**'s main door turn right and take a road which goes down the left hand side of the **post office**.

> The **Church at Châtel Montagne** is one of the best examples of Auvergne Romanesque art. Its nave dates from the early 12th century, whereas its chapels and entrance were constructed later in that century. The church, named for Our Lady, still has its original dome and some painted murals inside dating back to the 12th and 13th centuries.
>
> The church was sold off during the French Revolution for use as a warehouse for saltpetre.

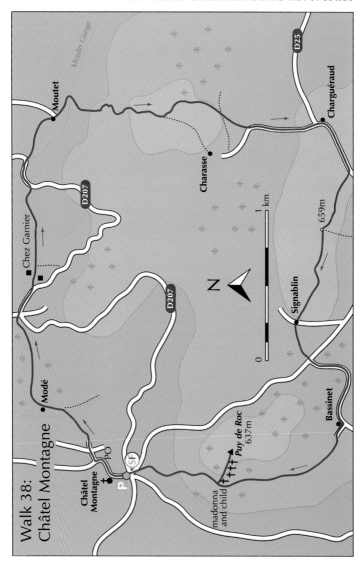

Walk 38:
Châtel Montagne

Notre-Dame de Châtel Montagne in the evening sun

Ignore a small track which leaves the road immediately right but take the next signposted track which veers off slightly rightwards. There are yellow and blue waymarkers here as the track dips steeply down to a stream. Cross a small stone bridge and turn left on another track, passing the house **Modé** after 50m. Climb from here and keep following the track for 500m until meeting the main **D207** road. Here turn left along the road for 300m then branch left at a signpost for **Chez Garnier**, and take the surfaced track down the hill through some buildings. Where the surfaced track turns right to rejoin the road head straight on along a little-used grassy path with waymarkers. This path is bordered by hedges.

After 500m reach the **D207** once more. Turn left along this for 200m. Just after crossing a bridge turn right on a path signposted to Moutet, following yellow and blue waymarkers. The path delves through a lovely tunnel of trees here and reaches the tranquil hamlet of **Moutet**, where there is a cross. Turn right by the cross on a track with a GR3 sign. Follow this for 300m downhill to the small **Moulin Gonge** river, to cross and ascend through a pleasant mixture of pretty farmland and ancient deciduous woodland of oak and chestnut. A long gradual climb eventually brings you to a fork where our route branches left. Stay on this well maintained gravelly track and ignore some confusing 'X' markings that denote defunct alternatives. Continue to a crossroads where the main way appears to be right but here go straight on, following an easily missable path uphill to join a minor road. Head left into the village of **Charguéraud**. ▶ Here turn right along the main **D25** road for 200m. Opposite a **cross** on the left take a track uphill to your right.

Here there is a small café.

Follow yellow waymarkers passing two small buildings, climbing over a hill (superb panorama) and descend towards the Signablin hamlet. Join a surfaced lane and turn left into **Signablin**. While passing through the settlement look for a waymarker that marks a track right (downhill) out of the village to meet the **D25** road, again at a **cross**. Head straight across this taking a minor road for 700m to the hamlet of **Bassinet**. Ignore the first track going right uphill opposite the first building of the sleepy hamlet, but take the next right which is signposted to Puy

Following the line of crosses up Puy de Roc

The track offers pleasant hiking while contouring the hillside.

de Roc. ◀ At a **Madonna and child statue** on the brow of a hill take a path climbing steadily right to the summit of **Puy de Roc**, only 200m away and well worth the detour. A line of unusual **crosses** leads to an orientation table.

Retrace your steps back to the Madonna and go right to reach **Châtel Montagne**.

WALK 39
Rocher St Vincent

Start/Finish	Lavoine
Distance	8km
Total Ascent	230m
Difficulty	2
Time	2hrs 30min
Highest Point	960m
Map	IGN 1:25,000 Sheet 2730O *Le Mayet de Montagne*
Public Transport	Limited bus service to Lavoine from Vichy
Parking	Ample parking in Lavoine

The Rocher St Vincent is one of the gems of the Montagne Bourbonnaise, and the recent decision to place a series of wind turbines close to its summit has left many locals fuming. For the visitor, however, this does not detract from a wonderful excursion immersed in local history, from cliff-top castles and eccentric timepieces to evidence of salt smugglers. The many crags of the Rocher are popular with local rock climbers.

Start at the attractive village of **Lavoine**, which boasts a wonderful little **church** with a clock, the obligatory war memorial, ample parking, an auberge and public toilets. Take time to note the strange wheel shaped clock in the centre of the village.

The **Horloge wheel** in Lavoine was in fact one of only three 'water and marbles' clocks in the world

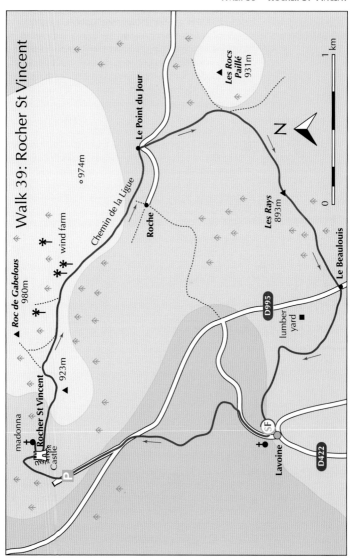

Walk 39: Rocher St Vincent

Roc de Gabelous 980m

wind farm

o 974m

Chemin de la Ligue

Le Point du Jour

Les Rocs Paillé 931m

N

1 km

0

Roche

Les Rays 893m

Le Beaulouis

D995

lumber yard

923m

D422

Rocher St Vincent

madonna

Castle

P

SF

Lavoine

which functioned by combining water and wood with precise measurements. A chute of water made the wheel rotate and water ran down via a pulley system to raise an arm, allowing exactly one wooden marble per minute to roll to the ground. At the sixtieth minute a system of counterweights signalled one hour had passed and the last marble had a special code on it to tell the exact hour.

Leave Lavoine by hiking down the road past the church. Just after the graveyard take a track branching off left (downhill) and pass a wrought iron cross. After 500m meet a small road and turn right (uphill) to reach the **D995** road. You will have to trudge along this for 100m until the taking the signed Rocher St Vincent turn off. This leads to a **parking area** with two picnic benches. Take the signed footpath to the Rocher.

The church at Lavoine with the Rocher beyond

Eventually this draws you to a clearing at the back NW side of the **Rocher St Vincent**. On the left is a statue of the **Madonna** vanquishing a snake on top of a smaller

rock. To reach the popular **summit** of the Rocher take the little path to your right. It is steep and a little exposed in parts, but will not trouble even the most timid of hikers.

The Rocher St Vincent

From the rocky summit return down to the clearing and turn right, looking out for a GR3 marker on a rock. Continue downhill through sparse woods

After 40m reach a fork in the path. Take the left way here and continue, finding the path joined by various

ROCHER ST VINCENT

The Rocher St Vincent is an imposing volcanic mass comprising two main buttresses separated by a grassy trough. Atop a minor buttress the Virgin Mary looks out and oversees the safety of the people of the Montagne Bourbonnaise. Another buttress boasts the remains of the small castle of Pyramont. The ruin on the S side is incredibly perched and it is easy to imagine an ancient game of King of the Castle taking place here. Legend has it that the castle's keep sat on the summit of the highest rock. Residents of Ferriéres then honoured a Spanish preacher called Vincent Ferrier who travelled to the region by building a chapel and statue on the Rocher but these have long gone and only the statue of this 'Saint' Vincent remains in the church at Ferriéres. ▶

Other rocks are viewed through the tree canopy along with Lavoine and its graveyard and Ferriéres further down the Sichon valley to the NW. Due south the forested skyline includes the high point of Allier, Puy de Montoncel (1287m, but not worth the walk as it offers no views, although an excellent Nordic ski centre does open there in winter).

forest tracks and head very gradually uphill to meet an obvious wide path coming in from the left. Head right uphill on this over the **923m spot height**. After 500m the GR3 veers off left towards **Roc de Gabelous** (a possible detour) but we continue straight on following a PR sign.

Gain the crest of the ridge at the newly-established and controversial **wind farm** and here go right down an obvious massive track, part of the **Chemin de la Ligue**, and pass a small electricity building and the hamlet of **Roche** (894m) to your right.

THE CHEMIN DE LA LIGUE

The Chemin de la Ligue was established by Greek and Roman merchants to link the Mediterranean and north coasts to move pewter necessary in the manufacturing of bronze. Later in the 16th century it was used by *La Ligue* – the Catholic army – during religious wars against the Protestants. The famous bandit Mandrin similarly used the route during his murderous campaign in the area. In the 18th century salt smugglers avoiding the *Gabelle* salt tax used the path but were often caught by the *Gabelous* – a special salt police. The Roc du Gabelous just off route commemorates this unsavoury business!

The route eventually enters another hamlet, **Le Point du Jour**. Follow a surfaced road for only 30m, then take a track rightwards with a yellow and blue waymarker. When a crossroads is met turn right along a track. A further track comes off left near **Les Rays**, but ignore this and amble along the lovely grassy track downhill to **le Beaulouis**. Here cross the **D995** road and pick up a track on the other side taking the first option going right. You will get views of the Rocher and nearby logging works during the 1km hike back to **Lavoine**.

WALK 40
The Cascade de la Pisserote

Start/Finish	Le Verger
Distance	4.5km
Total Ascent	90m
Difficulty	1
Time	1hr 15mins
Highest Point	700m
Map	IGN 1:25,000 Sheet 2730E *St Just/Monts de la Madeleine*
Parking	Parking area signed off the D26 Arfeuilles road

As one of the shortest excursions in this book, the Pisserote waterfalls make a pleasant objective for a short afternoon walk. This is a popular outing, though fewer walkers continue upstream from the falls to visit the abandoned mill. The popularity of the Pisserote seems to be spurred on by gushing descriptions in various pieces of local literature quoting its waters as 'impetuous' and 'magnificent'. Added to this, a widely known legend has grown up around the origins of the falls – see box below.

You might be forgiven for expecting a trip to the French equivalent of the Niagara when in fact the falls are a pretty excuse for an amble though tranquil pastoral scenery and deciduous woods. Keep expectations realistic and you won't be disappointed. This area of the Montagne Bourbonnaise gives the perfect impression of sleepy rural France. The nearest villages in which to hunt refreshment and accommodation are Arfeuilles, St Nicolas des Biefs and Châtel Montagne.

Start at the crossroads just before the hamlet of **le Verger**, where there is a water trough. Follow yellow waymarkers into the hamlet of le Verger down a small road signposted with a dead end sign. ▶ The route becomes a track and later a narrower path which passes right of a small **pond**. After 350m ignore a fork to the right and head straight on the wide path, eventually descending into a more dense forest, following an old stone wall. The path leads down to the **Barbenan river**, which is crossed by a decrepit wooden bridge.

The cascade is well signposted through the twists and turns of the hamlet.

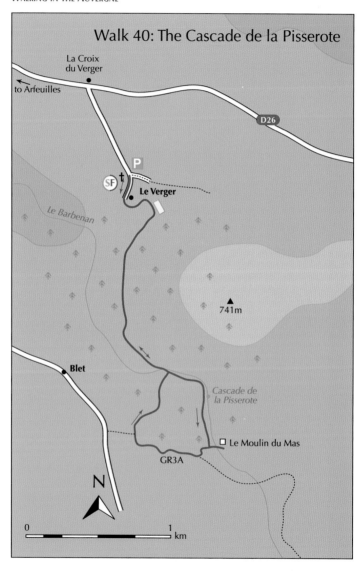

Walk 40: The Cascade de la Pisserote

La Croix
du Verger

to Arfeuilles

D26

P

SF ✝

Le Verger

Le Barbenan

▲
741m

Blet

*Cascade de
la Pisserote*

☐ Le Moulin du Mas

GR3A

N

0   1
                    km

Follow the river upstream to the **Cascade de la Pisserote**. The first of the falls is the largest but several more pleasant mini-cascades and pools can be discovered by clambering further up the eroded path beside the river's right bank marked with yellow or scrambling onto the rocks themselves. ▶

These rocks can be slippy after wet weather.

THE LEGEND OF THE PISSEROTE

The turbulence of the water had its origins thousands of years ago, when it was born in a circular granite basin called a *gour* where the cold waters of a torrent whirled. The popular belief attributed the formation of this *gour* to the power of fairies. No one knew the depth of the gour and a number of men and animals perished by falling into its waters. One day an old woman from a neighbouring village decided to unlock the secrets of the *gour*. She spun an interminable length of wool. She then attached a stone to the end and released it into the *gour* but the stone could not reach the bottom. The villagers decided to take action to prevent any further drownings. Numerous carts full of stones were pulled along the path beside the river by cattle. The contents of the carts were emptied into the *gour* and gradually it was filled. There was never another accident. Since that day the waterfall has become angry, throwing raging water against the rocks, trying to hurl them from the valley and recreate the dreaded *gour*!

The path continues to weave its way up round boulders and root systems on the right side of the river until 500m later a bridge to **le Moulin du Mas** is reached, near to a strange tree with horizontal double trunks blocking the path. Cross the bridge to view an old iron water wheel then double back across the river to find a return route.

On the opposite side to the mill an obscure path cuts steeply uphill through the trees. Various options exist but after 80m a clearer path is reached, signposting a route back to the Pisserote. Continue on this to reach the **GR3A** trail, marked with red and white signs. Follow this rightwards on a wide track through more open woodland and fields. In 600m a clear switchback downhill marked 'VTT' is taken. This leads steeply downhill and splits once where the left hand of two options should be taken to

The lower cascade of the Pisserote

reach the decrepit bridge near the Pisserote. Retrace the outbound route back to **le Verger**.

WALK 41

The Plateau de la Verrerie and its Tourbière

Start/Finish	St Nicolas des Biefs
Distance	7km
Total Ascent	170m
Difficulty	1
Time	1hr 50mins
Highest Point	1042m
Map	IGN 1:25,000 Sheet 2730E *St Just/Monts de la Madeleine*

This is a gentle afternoon walk, the principal highlights of which are the extensive views from the plateau. A clear day makes the best of the route and allows appreciation of the deep Loire valley and Forez plains, the distant spread of Roanne and faint alpine summits, including Mont Blanc, visible to the east. The plateau itself, named after the local glassblowing tradition, appears bland at first sight, but is in fact a *tourbière* or ancient volcanic lake, now a complex marshy ecosystem teaming with lizards and butterflies on hot days.

St Nicolas has a long tradition of master glassmaking dating back to the 17th century – the time of Louis XIV. This is represented in an informative Museé de Verrerie in the village. There were 18 glass kilns in the area, fed by the sand of the local rivers. Good examples of this local craft can be found in the beautiful stained glass windows of St Nicolas' church.

From the parking area behind the **church** head downhill to the D477 road. Cross the bridge on the bend and immediately take a rough track opposite the graveyard ascending right. After 500m reach a **cross** at a triangular crossroads with some houses. Take the right hand fork and then the second path left following a yellow and blue marker. The path eventually exits the forest and goes through brush and bracken curving leftwards to **la Grand Croix**, a lonely marker on the plateau. At the cross the track heads E, passing a covered reservoir 200m to your left. On joining the **D478** road, turn left for 100m to the Roc du Vacher **parking area**. From

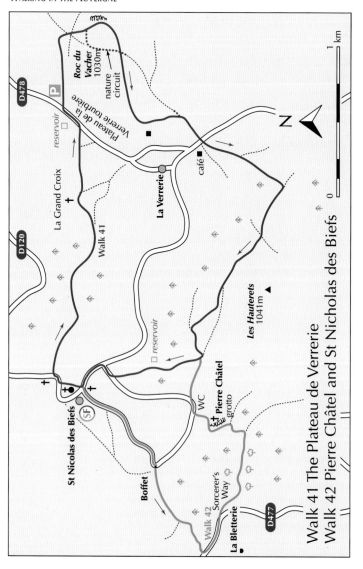

Walk 41 The Plateau de Verrerie
Walk 42 Pierre Châtel and St Nicholas des Biefs

the car park a lovely sandy track leads up to the rock through heather.

THE PLATEAU DE LA VERRERIE

The plateau is a tourbière – an ancient lake which has now become a bog formed over thousands of years by layer upon layer of decomposing vegetation settling in the damp depression. Here copious varieties of moss flourish and pollen, plant debris and fossils have lain undisturbed for millennia. Scientists have used samples from this area to gather invaluable data about the flora, fauna and climate of a bygone era. Drosera, a carnivorous plant used in medicine, also flourishes in the area.

Join the GR3A path after 200m heading straight on and following a sign to the **Roc du Vacher**. ▸

An orientation table makes sense of expansive vistas.

The **Roc du Vacher** was so called because the cowherds who set their cattle grazing on the deforested plateau used the rock for shelter from the wind. Local legend has it that the rocks were used as boules by giants.

From the table head downhill a little way, ignoring the GR trail coming off left: instead descend 40m to a pleasant picnicking spot. Follow the path down to a T junction, where the main route heads left.

Trying to spot Mont Blanc from atop the Roc du Vacher

Walking through the sleepy village of St Nicolas

There is a worthwhile **deviation on a nature circuit** of gangplanks where lizards and rare butterflies can often be spotted: to check this out, go right for 300m on the gangways leading to an overlook explaining the nature of the weird and wonderful ecosystem of the peaty *tourbière*. From the end of the gangplanks retrace your steps and continue on your original route.

After 50m downhill join a wider track and turn right (W), following yellow signs. This leads to the outskirts of **La Verrerie**, where a minor road is joined. Turn left here for 500m, heading up towards a mast at a cross-roads and a **café** on the D478/D420 junction. Go straight across the road and up the left side of the café to find a path. ◄ Continue up a grassy hill into the forest on a track. At a T junction of tracks turn right (NW) where views of the Monts Dômes and Dore are possible. A gradual descent follows yellow waymarkers towards St Nicolas. Another covered **reservoir** is passed and soon after a surfaced road leads into **St Nicolas**.

Here a board marks the extensive winter cross-country skiing in the area.

WALK 42

Pierre Châtel from St Nicolas des Biefs

Start/Finish	St Nicolas des Biefs
Distance	5km
Total Ascent	190m
Difficulty	1
Time	1hr 30mins
Highest Point	970m
Map	IGN 1:25,000 Sheet 2730E *St Just/Monts de la Madeleine*

This short route takes in some of the most interesting features around the pretty village of St Nicolas, which at 930m is the highest in the Allier region. A spooky amble through a glade of ancient twisted beech trees along the 'Sorcerer's Way' and a visit to a small grotto built into a cliff side are highlights of the walk. Superb panoramas of the Monts de la Madeleine are also gained from climbing to the airy vantage point of the rocky buttress of Pierre Châtel.

Park behind the village **church**. From the front of the church head up the road, taking the right fork at a give way sign and finding a white **cross** after 60m. Here turn right, signposted to Les Toines and Pierre Châtel. Follow yellow and blue waymarkers through the farming hamlet of **Boffet** on a small lane.

> Leaving Boffet the **controversial windmills** of the Rocher St Vincent come into view, and beyond them the Puy du Montoncel (1287m), the forested highpoint of the *département* of Allier.

When the main road takes a sharp bend to the left follow a signposted track straight on. After 100m the track forks – take the right hand option.

After 250m turn sharply left at the **D477** road, traversing above **la Bletterie**. A further 150m brings you to a bend, at which you take a wide track on your left. The

The twisted trees of the Sorcerer's Way

short **Sorcerer's Way** starts here. Follow the path between the crooked mossy trees to a crossroads and head straight on through the forest.

> The remarkably deformed **centenarian beeches** of the Sorcerer's Way once served as firewood. When cut, the stumps remained unscathed and the new growths from them were weakened to the point that the trunks themselves became more important and eventually took their tortuous forms of today.

After 150m the track forks. Take the left of the forks uphill and after another 150m a sign appears to suggest that you double back – ignore this and continue straight on until the track ends and two paths continue. Choose the left option here, climbing steeply. Just before reaching a decrepit wall at a stream, the path branches left following easily missed yellow waymarkers. This section ascends steeply to reach the foot of the large rock buttress of **Pierre Châtel**.

Looking out from the clifftops of Pierre Châtel

The observant hiker may spot **lines of bolts** weaving their way up the 40m high rock face of Pierre Châtel. These are sport climbing bolts and the Pierre Châtel is a popular location for Auvergne climbers.

Here follow the most worn path leftwards up to the rocks, followed by some precipitous narrow stone steps which lead to a **grotto** containing a statue of the Virgin Mary and child, a bench and a good viewpoint.

Once down from the grotto continue up the stony path beside the rocks. Turn right at the top turn to reach a steep but simple route to the exposed summit of the Rocher de la Croix, where a white wooden **cross** can be found along with extensive views of the Sapey and Besbre valleys. Having retraced your steps, follow waymarkers up to a grassy clearing then trend rightwards up to the Pierre Châtel picnic area, where there are **public toilets** and running water. ◄

Discreet free camping is tolerated here.

Go direct to the road from the toilet building and turn right for 30m, then come off left, taking a track straight up the hill. A further 250m along this turn left for a similar distance until reaching a small covered **reservoir**. Continue left of this and follow the road winding down to the village of **St Nicolas**.

APPENDIX A

Route summary table

The Cantal

No	Title	Start	Difficulty	Distance	Time
1	Puy de Niermont	Col de Serre	2	8km	2hrs 45mins
2	An Ascent of the Puy de Peyre Arse	La Graviére	3	14.5km	5–6 hrs (4hrs with escape route)
3	Puy Mary with Optional Excursion to Puy de la Tourte	Pas de Peyrol parking area on the D680	1 or 2	2.5 or 6.5km	50mins (+ 1½hrs for Puy de la Tourte)
4	Traverse of the Brèche de Rolland from Puy Mary to Peyre Arse	Pas de Peyrol parking area on the D680	3	9km	3hrs 30mins (alt route 2hrs 30mins)
5	Around Medieval Murat	Tourist office in main square of Murat	1	7km	2hrs 30mins
6	The Plomb du Cantal	Les Gardes near St Jacques des Blats	3	11km	4hrs 30mins (5hrs 15mins from St Jaques)
7	A Rombière Ramble	Parc de Volcans d'Auvergne parking between Pas de Peyrol and Mandailles	1	5km	1hr 20mins

No	Title	Start	Difficulty	Distance	Time
8	Puy Griou	Parc de Volcans d'Auvergne parking between Pas de Peyrol and Mandailles	3	12.5km	4hrs 30mins
9	Up the Usclade	Col du Pertus parking area off D317 St Jacques to Mandailles	2	7km	2hrs
10	The Elancèze	Col du Pertus parking area off D317 St Jacques to Mandailles	1 or 3	3 or 8km	1hr 15mins (longer circuit 3hrs)
11	Puy Violent and the Shadow Rock	Récusset on the D37 off the N side of the D680 Pas de Peyrol road	3	14km	5hrs
12	Roches Taillade and Roc d'Hozières	Parking area on D17 2km SW of Pas de Peyrol	1 or 2	6km	1hr 45mins (2hrs 15mins with Taillade)
13	Circuit of Puy Chavaroche	Mandailles	3	13km	4hrs 30mins–5hrs
14	St Cirgues de Jordanne – Southern circuit	Church in St Cirgues de Jordanne	1	6.5km	2hrs 15mins
15	St Cirgues de Jordanne – Northern circuit	Church in St Cirgues de Jordanne	1	6.5km	2hrs 15mins

Châine des Puys (Monts Dômes)

No	Title	Start	Difficulty	Distance	Time
16	Puy de Dôme	Col de Ceyssat	2	7.5km	2hrs 15mins
17	Puys Lassolas and de la Vache	Car park 4km NE along the D5 from the D5/N89 junction	2	4km	1hr 30mins
18	Around Orcival	St Bonnet près Orcival on D27 accessed from N89	2	11.5km	3hrs 15mins
19	Puy des Gouttes	Parking area 500m E of D559/ D941 roundabout	1	6km	1hr 45mins
20	The Crater of Puy Pariou	Parking area off D941 Clermont-Pontgibaud road nr Orcines	1	6.5km	2hrs
21	The Water of Volvic	Volvic Source's free visitor centre	1 or 3	5 or 15km	1hr 30min (longer circuit 5hrs)

The Monts Dore

No	Title	Start	Difficulty	Distance	Time
22	The Great Horseshoe: Puy de Sancy from Mont-Dore	Mont-Dore funicular station on W side of town centre (Station du Mont-Dore for shorter walk)	3 or 2	8 or 16.5km	6hrs (shorter walk 3hrs 15mins)
23	Up the Chaudefour Valley to Puys Sancy and Ferrand	Chaudefour Valley parking area on the D36 from Besse-en-Chandesse	3	13km	5hrs
24	Around Lake Pavin	Large parking area off the D149 5km from Besse-en-Chandesse	1	4km	1hr 20mins
25	Connecting the Cascades of Puy d'Angle	Prends-toi-Garde at the N side of Mont-Dore	3	16km	5hrs 30mins
26	The Tuilière and Sanadoire rocks	Parking area off the D80 4km from the Col de Guéry	2 or 1	7km	2hrs–2hrs 20mins
27	A Tour of the Curiosities of St Nectaire	St Nectaire church above the village off the D150	1	9km	3hrs
28	Lake Guéry and the Banne d'Ordanche	Maison de la Flore ski centre	2	12km	4hrs (4hrs 30mins with Puy Loup)

The Haute-Loire: Livradois Forez and Velay

No	Title	Start	Difficulty	Distance	Time
29	Around Chaise-Dieu and the Senouire	La Chaise-Dieu abbey parking area off N102 N of le Puy	1	4.5km	1hr 30mins
30	The Gorges of the Loire	Lavoûte-sur-Loire, 11km N of le Puy	2	11km	3hrs 40mins
31	A Circuit of Allègre	Allègre	1	6km	1hr 30mins
32	Mont Bar from Allègre	Allègre	1	4km	1hr 15mins
33	Domeyrat and the Senouire	Domeyrat	1	5.5km	1hr 40mins
34	Vieille Brioude and the Ceroux	Place de la Croix de Pres, Vieille Brioude	2	11km	3hrs 15mins
35	Lavaudieu Abbey and the Senouire	Lavaudieu village between Paulhaguet and Brioude on the N102 Le Puy to Clermont road	2	10km	2hrs 45mins

The Montagne Bourbonnaise

No	Title	Start	Difficulty	Distance	Time
36	The Ruins of Montgilbert	Ferriéres sur Sichon War Memorial	2	10km	3–3½hrs
37	Milling around the Mills	Ferriéres sur Sichon War Memorial	1	10km	3hrs
38	Around Châtel Montagne and the Puy de Roc	Châtel Montagne church	1	9km	2hrs 45mins
39	Rocher St Vincent	Lavoine	2	8km	2hrs 30mins
40	The Cascade de la Pisserote	Le Verger	1	4.5km	1hr 15mins
41	The Plateau de la Verrerie and its Tourbière	St Nicolas des Biefs	1	7km	1hr 50mins
42	Pierre Châtel from St Nicolas des Biefs	St Nicolas des Biefs	1	5km	1hr 30mins

APPENDIX B
Glossary of French walking terms

French	English	French	English
accueil	ticket booth	*crête*	ridge crest
aiguille	rock needle	*croix*	cross
alimentation	food shop	*dangereux/se*	dangerous
aller/retour	return trip	*départ*	starting point
auberge	guest house/	*difficile*	difficult
	restaurant	*droit*	right
autobus	bus	*douche*	shower
autostop	hitchhiking	*eau*	water
balade	short walk	*eau potable*	drinking water
balisé	waymarked	*église*	church
barrage	dam	*épicerie*	grocery
basilique	basilica	*escalade*	climbing
belvedere	lookout	*étang*	tarn
bois	wood	*facile*	easy
borne	boundary stone	*fermé*	closed
bouche	mouth	*fleuve*	river
boulangerie	bakery	*fontaine*	fountain
buron	cowherd's	*forêt*	forest
	dwelling	*gare*	train station
buvette	snack bar	*gauche*	left
calvaire	cross (usually	*gendarme*	free-standing
	on hill top, as in		rock obelisk
	Calvary)	*gîte*	self catering
carte	map	*gîte d'étape*	walking hostel
cascade	waterfall	*grotte*	cave
cathédrale	cathedral	*hameau*	hamlet
chambre	room	*hébergement*	accommodation
chambre d'hôte	bed and	*horaire*	timetable
	breakfast	*itinéraire*	route
chasse	hunting	*lac*	lake
château	castle	*libre*	free
chemin	path	*location*	for rent
chemin de fer	railway	*mairie*	town hall
col	mountain pass	*maison*	house

French	English	French	English
mont/montagne	mountain	rocher/roc	rock
moulin	mill	route	road
méteo	weather	ruisseau	stream
navette	minibus	sac á dos	rucksack
neige	snow	sanglier	wild boar
orage	storm	secours	help
ouvert	open	sentier	route
pain	bread	sommet	peak
pierre	stone	source	spring
piscine	pool	tarif	fare
piste	ski run	thermes	spa
pluie	rain	tour	tower
pont	bridge	tourbière	marshy crater lake
prix	price		
puy	volcanic summit	vallée	valley
randonée pedestre	walking	verger	orchard
refuge	refuge	ville	town
riviére	river	volcan	volcano

APPENDIX C
Further reading

Aarnio, Hanu *Butterflies of Europe: A photographic guide* (A&C Black, 2009)

Anglade, Jean *L'Auvergne de Jean Anglade* (Editions de Borée, 2007)

Aston, S C *Peirol: Troubadour of Auvergne* (Cambridge University Press, 2010)

Bellier, Michel and Chapuis, Claude *Vins du Massif Central* (Timée-éditions, 2009)

Castle, Alan *The Grand Traverse of the Massif Central* (Cicerone Press, 2010)

Cattermole, Peter *Auvergne (Classic Geology in Europe)* (Terra Publishing, 2001)

Costello, Louisa Stuart *A Pilgrimage to Auvergne, from Picardy to Le Velay* (Bibliobazaar, 2009)

De Kantzow, Herbert *Summer Days in Auvergne* (Adamant Media Corporation, 2004)

Despesse, Jean-Louis *Auvergne Geoguide* (Guides Gallimard, 2012)

Gosling, Frances Marion *Auvergne and its People* (Adamant Media Corporation, 1911)

Graham, Peter *Mourjou: The Life and Food of an Auvergne Village* (Prospect Books, 2003)

Knowles, Peter *White Water Massif Central* (Rivers Publishing UK, 2002)

Hume, Rob *RSPB Birds of Britain and Europe* (Dorling Kindersley, 2011)

Huon, Olivier *Balades Nature dans les Volcans d'Auvergne* (Dakota Editions, 2012)

Michelin Green Guide *Auvergne Rhone Valley*, 7th Edition (Michelin Green Guides, 2013)

Olivier, Luc *L'Auvergne* (Ouest-France, 2008)

Ophuls, Marcel, Hoffman, Stanley and Johnston, Mireille *The Sorrow and the Pity: Chronicle of a French city under the German occupation* (pb: Paladin, 1974)

Sorrow and the Pity DVD starring Georges Bidault, Matthäus Bleibinger, Charles Braun et al (Arrow, 2004)

Sutton, David and Emberson, Colin *Green Guide to Wild Flowers of Britain and Europe* (New Holland, 2001)

Svenson, Lars *Collins Bird Guide to Britain and Europe* (Collins, 2010)

Talbot, Rosaline *Guide de Merveilles de Nature* (Arthaud, 2007)

Weld, Charles Richard *Auvergne, Piedmont, and Savoy: A Summer Ramble* (Bilbiobazaar, 2009)

APPENDIX D
Useful contacts

General
The international dialling code for France is 0033.

Emergency
Call 112 or 18 for fire services and 17 for police.

Tourist information
www.auvergne-tourisme.info based at 44 Av des Etats-Unis

Clermont-Ferrand runs tours and books accommodation 08 1082 7828

Regional Tourist Board www.maisondelauvergne.com 04 7329 4949 or
www.auvergnevacances.com 04 7107 4154

French Walking Federation www.ffrandonee.fr 01 4489 9393

Auvergne walking committee www.auvergnerando.com 04 7391 9401

Parc Naturel Régional des Volcans d'Auvergne
www.parc-volcans-auvergne.com 04 7365 6400

Jardins du Massif Central
Botanical gardens and arboretums
www.jardinsmassifcentral.com 04 7395 0071

Maps
IGN www.ign.fr produce and sell topographical maps and cycling guides

Chamina produce local walking routes and guides
www.chamina.com 04 7392 8144

Weather
www.meteo.fr or call 03 50

Transport
Trains www.sncf.com or www.ter-sncf.com/auvergne
or call 36 35 or 08 9167 0068

Airport at Clermont-Ferrand 04 7362 7100

Accommodation
Gîtes www.gites-refuges.com and en.gites-de-france.com (in English)

Walkers' accommodation www.rando-accueil.com

Horseriding
www.chevalfrance.org

Committee for Equestrian Tourism
www.cdte63.com 04 7342 2246

Fishing
www.auvergne.angloinfo.com has good suggestions for fishing and other sports

Ecotourism
www.stationverte.com

Rock climbing
www.ffme.fr 06 2682 7863

Tourist driving itineraries
The Cheese Route www.fromages-aoc-auvergne.com 04 7148 6615

Châteaux Route www.route-chateaux-auvergne.org 04 7319 1216

Crafts of the Livradois Forez Route www.routedesmetiers.com 04 7395 5804

Spa Route www.villes-eaux.tm.fr 04 7334 7280

The Cantal

Tourist offices
Cantal www.cdt-cantal.fr 04 7163 8500

Puy Mary www.puymary.fr 06 0803 3510

Murat www.officedetourismepaysdemurat.com 04 7120 0947

Lioran www.lelioran.com 04 7149 5008

Mandailles 94 7147 9442

General information on history, activities and burons
www.cantalpassion.com

www.massifcantalienne.com

Skiing
Plomb du Cantal cable car and chairlift www.lelioran.com 04 7149 5009

Cross-country skiing www.leclaux-puymary.com 04 7178 9388

Doctors
Murat 04 7120 0970 and 04 7120 0852

Hospital
Murat 04 7120 3034

Gîtes bookings
www.gites-de-france-cantal.fr 04 7148 6420

Cycle hire
Murat www.caldera-bike.com 04 7120 2184

Horseriding
www.chevalrandonee.com

Paragliding
Puy Mary www.parapente-puy-mary.com 04 7178 9521

Other Cantal summits www.cantalairlibre.com 06 7801 6951

Family-friendly adventure
Adventure centre in Lioran
www.lioran-aventure.com 06 7497 4094

The Chaîne de Puys (Monts Dômes) and Monts Dore

General tourist office
www.planetepuydedome.com 04 7342 2250

Town tourist offices
Orcival 04 7365 8977

Mont-Dore 04 7365 5313

Saint Nectaire 04 7388 5086

Murat www.murat.fr 04 7120 0380

Accommodation
www.sancy-volcans.com 04 7365 3600

Skiing infomation
Sancy massif www.sancy.com 04 7321 5387

Mont-Dore Bureau de Montagne 04 7365 0774

Puy de Sancy www.sancy.com
chairlift 04 7365 0223
funicular 04 7365 0125

Family-friendly adventure
Vulcania is a volcano-themed family park
www.vulcania.com 08 2082 7828

Volcan de Lemptegy is a family-friendly tour inside a volcano
www.auvergne-volcan.com 04 7362 2325

Spas
Mont-Dore 04 7365 0510, la Bourboule 04 7381 2100

Volvic visitor centre
www.espaceinfo.volvic.fr 04 7364 5124

Haute-Loire: Livradois Forez and Velay

General tourist office
Parc Naturel Régional Livradois-Forez
www.parc-livradois-forez.org 04 7395 5757

Tourist office of the Haute-Loire in le Puy
www.mididelauvergne.com 04 7107 4154

Town tourist offices
Saint Paulien 04 7100 5001

Thiers www.thiers-tourisme.fr 04 7380 6565

Chaise-Dieu www.la-chaise-dieu.info 04 7100 0116

Allègre www.cc-portes-auvergne.fr 04 7100 7252

Brioude and Lavaudieu
www.ot-brioude.fr 04 7174 9749 or 04 7176 4600

Walking association for the Haute-Loire
www.lacroiseedeschemins.com 04 7104 1595

Villages of the Chaise-Dieu plateau association
www.cc-plateau-chaisedieu.fr 04 7100 0822

Cycling
Road cycling information 04 7109 7168

Mountain biking information
ambertvtt.free.fr 04 7382 6844

Cross-country skiing
www.ski-cretes-du-forez.org 04 7382 0004

Scenic train rides
www.agrivap.fr 04 7382 4388

The Montagne Bourbonnaise

General tourist office
Comité Départmental de Tourisme de l'Allier is the area's tourist board
www.allier-tourisme.com 04 7046 8150

Conseil Général de l'Allier is the general council of Allier 04 7034 4003

Town tourist offices
Mayet de Montagne www.mayet-montagne.auvergne.net 04 7059 3840

Ferriéres sur Sichon www.ferrieres-sur-sichon.fr 04 7041 1489

Châtel Montagne 04 7059 3789

Vichy www.vichy-tourisme.com 04 7098 7194

Doctors
Ferriéres 04 7041 1380

Laprugne 04 7059 7707

Hospital
Vichy 04 7097 3333

Skiing
Downhill at Laprugne www.logedesgardes.com 04 7056 4444

Cross-country at Lavoine 04 7096 0110 and at St Nicolas des Biefs 04 7056 4995

Mountain Biking
www.boisnoirs.fr

Accommodation
Gîtes de l'Allier reservations 04 7046 8160

Weather
Allier weather information line 08 3668 0203

Rock climbing
Club Grimpamicale www.grimpamicale.fr can give you information about rock climbing in the Montagne Bourbonnaise

Museum
Musée de Glozel in Ferriéres is a museum of archaeological finds
www.museedeglozel.com

See the Introduction for further information about accommodation in particular areas.

NOTES

LISTING OF CICERONE GUIDES

Walking in the Dordogne
Walking in the Haute Savoie
   North & South
Walking in the Languedoc
Walking in the Tarentaise and
   Beaufortain Alps
Walking on Corsica

GERMANY

Germany's Romantic Road
Walking in the Bavarian Alps
Walking in the Harz Mountains
Walking the River Rhine Trail

HIMALAYA

Annapurna
Bhutan
Everest: A Trekker's Guide
Garhwal and Kumaon: A
   Trekker's and Visitor's Guide
Kangchenjunga: A Trekker's
   Guide
Langtang with Gosainkund and
   Helambu: A Trekker's Guide
Manaslu: A Trekker's Guide
The Mount Kailash Trek
Trekking in Ladakh

ICELAND & GREENLAND

Trekking in Greenland
Walking and Trekking in Iceland

IRELAND

Irish Coastal Walks
The Irish Coast to Coast Walk
The Mountains of Ireland

ITALY

Gran Paradiso
Sibillini National Park
Stelvio National Park
Shorter Walks in the Dolomites
Through the Italian Alps
Trekking in the Apennines
Trekking in the Dolomites
Via Ferratas of the Italian
   Dolomites: Vols 1 & 2
Walking in Abruzzo
Walking in Sardinia
Walking in Sicily
Walking in the Central Italian
   Alps
Walking in the Dolomites
Walking in Tuscany
Walking on the Amalfi Coast
Walking the Italian Lakes

MEDITERRANEAN

Jordan – Walks, Treks, Caves,
   Climbs and Canyons
The Ala Dag
The High Mountains of Crete
The Mountains of Greece
Treks and Climbs in Wadi Rum,
   Jordan
Walking in Malta
Western Crete

NORTH AMERICA

British Columbia
The Grand Canyon
The John Muir Trail
The Pacific Crest Trail

SOUTH AMERICA

Aconcagua and the Southern
   Andes
Torres del Paine

SCANDINAVIA

Walking in Norway

SLOVENIA, CROATIA AND
MONTENEGRO

The Julian Alps of Slovenia
The Mountains of Montenegro
Trekking in Slovenia
Walking in Croatia
Walking in Slovenia: The
   Karavanke

SPAIN AND PORTUGAL

Costa Blanca: West
Mountain Walking in Southern
   Catalunya
The Mountains of Central Spain
The Northern Caminos
Trekking through Mallorca
Walking in Madeira
Walking in Mallorca
Walking in the Algarve
Walking in the Cordillera
   Cantabrica
Walking in the Sierra Nevada
Walking on La Gomera and El
   Hierro
Walking on La Palma
Walking on Tenerife
Walks and Climbs in the Picos
   de Europa

SWITZERLAND

Alpine Pass Route
Canyoning in the Alps

Central Switzerland
The Bernese Alps
The Swiss Alps
Tour of the Jungfrau Region
Walking in the Valais
Walking in Ticino
Walks in the Engadine

TECHNIQUES

Geocaching in the UK
Indoor Climbing
Lightweight Camping
Map and Compass
Mountain Weather
Moveable Feasts
Outdoor Photography
Polar Exploration
Rock Climbing
Sport Climbing
The Book of the Bivvy
The Hillwalker's Guide to
   Mountaineering
The Hillwalker's Manual

MINI GUIDES

Avalanche!
Navigating with a GPS
Navigation
Pocket First Aid and Wilderness
   Medicine
Snow

For full information on all
our guides, and to order
books and eBooks, visit our
website:
www.cicerone.co.uk.

Walking – Trekking – Mountaineering – Climbing – Cycling

Over 40 years, Cicerone have built up an outstanding collection of 300 guides, inspiring all sorts of amazing adventures.

Every guide comes from extensive exploration and research by our expert authors, all with a passion for their subjects. They are frequently praised, endorsed and used by clubs, instructors and outdoor organisations.

All our titles can now be bought as **e-books** and many as iPad and Kindle files and we will continue to make all our guides available for these and many other devices.

Our website shows any **new information** we've received since a book was published. Please do let us know if you find anything has changed, so that we can pass on the latest details. On our **website** you'll also find some great ideas and lots of information, including sample chapters, contents lists, reviews, articles and a photo gallery.

It's easy to keep in touch with what's going on at Cicerone, by getting our monthly **free e-newsletter**, which is full of offers, competitions, up-to-date information and topical articles. You can subscribe on our home page and also follow us on **Facebook** and **Twitter**, as well as our **blog**.

Cicerone – the very best guides for exploring the world.

CICERONE

2 Police Square Milnthorpe Cumbria LA7 7PY
Tel: 015395 62069 info@cicerone.co.uk
www.cicerone.co.uk